KNOCK, KNOCK!

Also By William Hartston

The Encyclopaedia of Everything Else
Numb and Number
The Bumper Book of Things that Nobody Knows
A Brief History of Puzzles
Sloths
The Kings of Chess
Teach Yourself Chess
Chess: The Making of the Musical
How to Cheat at Chess
Soft Pawn
The Drunken Goldfish
How Was it For You, Professor?

WILLIAM HARTSTON

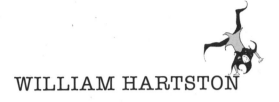

KNOCK, KNOCK!

In Pursuit of a Grand Unified Theory of Humour

WATKINS
Sharing Wisdom
Since 1893

Knock, Knock
William Hartston

First published in the UK and USA in 2023 by
Watkins, an imprint of Watkins Media Limited
Unit 11, Shepperton House, 83–93 Shepperton Road
London N1 3DF

enquiries@watkinspublishing.com

1 2 3 4 5 6 7 8 9 10

Typeset by JCS Publishing Services Ltd
Printed in the United Kingdom by TJ Books Ltd

A CIP record for this book is available from the British Library

ISBN: 978-1-78678-732-3 (Paperback)

www.watkinspublishing.com

MIX
Paper from
responsible sources
FSC
www.fsc.org   FSC® C013056

"Common sense and a sense of humour are the same thing, moving at different speeds. A sense of humour is just common sense, dancing. Those who lack humour are without judgement and should be trusted with nothing."

Clive James (in a television review in
The Observer, 4 February 1979)

ABOUT THE AUTHOR

After reading maths at Cambridge, William Hartston became an industrial psychologist, developing personality tests for use in recruiting and placement in industry. While doing this, he played far too much chess, winning the British championship a couple of times, but when overtaken by a far more talented younger generation took the sensible decision to write about them rather than try to compete against them.

This led to a career in books and journalism, first at *The Independent*, then at the *Daily Express* where he has been writing the Beachcomber column of surreal humour for the past 25 years. He has also written several books on such diverse topics as chess, bizarre academic research, useless information, numbers and sloths.

Despite all this, he still hasn't decided what he wants to be when he grows up.

CONTENTS

ACKNOWLEDGMENTS

Quite apart from my indebtedness to Plato, Aristotle, Sigmund Freud and all the other philosophers and psychologists whose unconvincing writings about humour persuaded me of the need to write this book, there are two people in particular whom I must thank for providing help where I most needed it.

I am particularly grateful to Etan Ilfeld, who first suggested to me the idea of writing for Watkins and who provided constant encouragement and helpful suggestions as the work took shape. His suggestions, and those of others at Watkins, were very useful in helping the work develop some sort of coherent shape.

I am also enormously grateful to UCL neuropsychologist Aygun Badalova for her patient explanations of everything I did not understand in chapter six. All the confusion that remains in that section, however, is all my own work.

The index is also my own work and as I compiled it I became aware of the great number of academic papers I have referred to, as well as the vast number of comic writers and performers who have helped convince me that Plato and Aristotle got things wrong. Some 2,000 of these have been deemed worthy of entries in Wikipedia, of whom I have had mentioned only a handful who have been chosen toexemplify the points I try to make about the history of comedy. If I have not mentioned your particular favourites, I can only crave your forgiveness and assure you that I intensely admire, and usually laugh at, all of them.

INTRODUCTION

"Humour is a great way for us to have evolved so we don't have to hit each other with sticks."

Scott Weems, cognitive neuroscientist

"Humour is the best way to make the unbearable bearable."

Mary Ann Shaffer, writer

"Humour is the only form of communication in which a stimulus on a high level of complexity produces a stereotyped, predictable response on the physiological reflex level."

Encyclopaedia Britannica

"Self-deprecating humour is the best way to seduce women."

US study by Gil Greengross and others at the University of New Mexico in 2008

"Humour is not resigned, it is rebellious. It symbolises not only the triumph of the ego but also of the pleasure principle, which is able here to assert itself against the unkindness of the real circumstances."

Sigmund Freud, neurologist, 1928

"Humour is the most effective flirting strategy for long-term relationships and flings."

"Perceived Effectiveness of Flirtation Tactics", by
Leif Kennair et al. *Evolutionary Psychology*, 2022

"Humour is a funny thing – everyone knows it but no
one knows what it is."
Alan Roberts, author of *The Philosophy of Humour*, 2019

I suppose all of the above descriptions are right in a way, but it seems to me that the last one comes closest to the truth: we really do not know what humour is, or why humour is, or where it came from. Many years ago, I read a science-fiction story by Isaac Asimov called "Jokester" about a genius who was feeding jokes into a supercomputer to try to discover the origins of humour. Eventually, the computer tells him that humour in humans began as a psychological study imposed on us by extraterrestrials. When the scientist asks what the consequences will be of our discovering this answer, he is told that the experiment will end and we will never find anything funny again. And that is exactly what happens all over the world.

Well, we still do not know what humour really is or where it comes from or even what the true nature of the relationship between humour and laughter is, but thanks to the increasing sophistication of brain-scanning devices, we are at last beginning to discover what happens when we are moved to laughter.

So why, you may ask, am I writing this book if we, which includes me, still know so little? The fact is that I have always thought the best reason for writing any book is because you want to read it – and that certainly applied in this case. From the age of nine or ten, I was addicted to comedy shows on what we then called the BBC Home Service. Every Sunday afternoon, I would run downstairs to turn on the kitchen wireless and tune in to such programmes as *Ray's a Laugh* (not even noticing that the title was a dreadful pun) and *The Goon Show*, not really understanding why its surreal humour amused me so much, not aware of what surreal meant anyway, and not knowing why Spike Milligan saying "he's fallen in the water" in a silly voice always made me laugh.

In the interests of research and enjoying myself, I have therefore spent much time over the past few decades continuing to listen to radio comedy, watching comedians on television, following sitcoms which I have often found more sit than com, laughing at comic films and comic operas, and reading comic novels; and the more I have done so, the more I have come to realize that all attempts to explain humour are woefully incomplete.

Philosophers since the time of Plato and Aristotle have tried to make humour fit into their own theories about human nature, more often than not deciding that it can't be done, so humour must be denounced as a human weakness. Psychologists have tried to build up theories of humour to explain why certain things make us laugh, but their theories are usually inadequate and utterly humourless. Sigmund Freud's writings on the relationship between jokes and the unconscious mind is particularly unfunny and more than anything reveals how rarely his own unconscious must have laughed at anything.

Many others have written on the differences in humour between various cultures, or the vexed question of whether religions should encourage or prohibit humour, or the development of humour in infants, or the fact that rats giggle when you tickle them, but nobody, as far as I could tell, has ever tried to bring together all these disparate threads in an attempt to develop a Grand Unified Theory of Humour that could apply to them all. It is highly unlikely that this book will even take the first steps toward such a GUT-Humour, but at least I hope it will pose some pertinent questions.

Why do audiences predictably laugh at catchphrases when they generally do not laugh at jokes they have heard before?

Why are words with a K in them generally found to be funnier than words without a K? When is an absence of humour unexpected enough to be funny? Is humour steadily becoming more sophisticated or are its changes simply a matter of fashion? Why am I asking so many questions instead of just getting on with the book? Does anyone ever read introductions anyway?

Well, I just thought I'd try to explain what I'm trying to do in these pages, while keeping a proper balance between Clive James's "common sense" and "dancing". So let's get on with it.

PART ONE

HUMOUR IN THEORY

"It doesn't matter how beautiful your theory is, it doesn't matter how smart you are. If it doesn't agree with experiment, it's wrong."

Richard P. Feynman

I
NEW JOKES FOR OLD

"A serious and good philosophical work could be written that would consist entirely of jokes."

Ludwig Wittgenstein

This particular work is not primarily philosophical and I'll leave it to you to decide whether it's any good. Unlike many books on humour it doesn't consist entirely of jokes, so let's start with one anyway: "A dyslexic walked into a bra . . ." But we'll bump into that again later.

Funny thing, humour. It has been with us for thousands of years and has been studied by philosophers, psychologists, literary critics, anthropologists and even animal behaviourists, yet there are almost as many theories of humour as there are theorists. The trouble with philosophers is that jokes present them with a real problem: philosophy has its basis in logic; jokes have their basis in disrupting logic. Another problem is that once you've heard a joke, it ceases to be funny. You don't laugh the second time it is told to you. You may smile through the memory of your earlier reaction but you don't laugh out loud as you did before. That is why old jokes may be a good place to start.

As the children's author E. B. White brilliantly pointed out in the introduction to *A Subtreasury of American Humor* in 1941: "Humor can be dissected, as a frog can, but the thing dies in the process and the innards are discouraging to any but the pure scientific mind." Philosophers, however, are very difficult to discourage once their brains get hold of a subject, which may explain why they have come up with so many theories of humour, none of which quite seems to work.

As I have already suggested, theorizing is a rational process, while any recipe for humour must include at least a modicum of irrationality. Another part of the problem is that the theorists themselves take their task very seriously and humourlessly, which all too often makes it look as though they are missing the point. As we shall see later, Sigmund Freud's *The Joke and Its Relation to the Subconscious* is one of the least funny books ever.

Bearing this and E. B. White's froggy analogy in mind, I shall try to be gentle in the dissections of humour that follow, so let's get back to the dyslexic in our opening paragraph. Comprising only six words, this may claim to be the shortest self-contained joke in existence. As we shall see, there have certainly been shorter jokes, even down to a single word, but in general these demand a good deal of preliminary setting-up, either by words or actions. Our dyslexic joke, however, is more subtle: to appreciate its humour, one needs some knowledge of the history of the genre it represents.

First, one must appreciate that this is a development or even parody of the many jokes that begin with the words: "A man walks into a bar . . ." Second, one must perceive the lunatic logic that a man who has a tendency to get letters in the wrong order might confuse a bar with a bra. Third, but not least, there is the additional humour to be gained from imagining a bad speller walking innocently into a bra. And all that is encapsulated in six words. The humour may be seen as a complex result of history, culture and mild social incorrectness, but to do so would take most of the fun out of it.

To continue flogging this particular dead frog, we could also see it as a specific case of the evolution of a type of joke, but to what extent humour is subject to true evolution and how much our tastes in humour are mainly a matter of fashion is an open question. What has undoubtedly evolved, however, is the language of humour.

When the word "humour" first appeared in the English language in the 14th century, there was nothing funny about it. Following the anatomical beliefs of the ancient Greeks and Romans, it came from the Latin *humor*, meaning fluid, and referred to the four fluids believed to flow through our bodies. The humours were blood, phlegm, choler (yellow bile) and melancholy (black bile), and most ills of body or temperament were thought to be due to an imbalance between these humours. Being in "good humour" (a term first seen in 1571 according to the *Oxford English Dictionary*) thus meant a well-balanced personality in a relaxed mood, but it was not until the second half of the 18th century that the funny side of the word "humour" began to be generally appreciated.

"Comedy" also had an ancient and not particularly amusing start. For ancient Greek and Roman dramatists, and indeed in the rest of Europe until at least the 16th century, it was a catch-all term for any play that was not a tragedy. Aristophanes, who lived in Athens around 400 BC, may not have been the first writer in this genre but he was certainly the best known and most prolific. He is known to have written 40 comedies of which only 11 survive and the nature of their humour seems mainly to have been a combination of vicious political satire and scatological references to bodily functions, especially farting.

Around this time, the Greeks also had a Muse of comedy. Thalia, like the other eight Muses, was depicted as one of the daughters of Zeus and Mnemosyne and was also the Muse of idyllic poetry. She was often depicted carrying a comic theatrical mask, though what she was meant to have done with it was never made clear. According to some sources, besides her responsibilities to comedy and poetry, she also invented geometry, architectural science and agriculture, so she was clearly a very busy girl.

Aristotle, in his *Poetics* written in 335 BC, about 50 years after the death of Aristophanes, made the interesting point that comedy was never treated seriously because its origins lay in bawdy songs in phallic processions and fertility festivals. Unlike serious drama and poetry, its appeal lay in the light treatment of the base and ugly.

According to him, comedy aims at representing people as being worse than in real life, while tragedy treats them as better. "Comedy", he wrote, "consists in some defect or ugliness which is not painful or destructive."

Sadly, only the first volume of Aristotle's *Poetics* survives, which consists mainly of his thoughts about tragedy so only mentions comedy in passing to emphasize its contrast. "Of comedy", he says, "we will speak hereafter", but we do not know what he had to say. Various attempts have been made, from his other writings, to reconstruct what the lost part of Aristotle's *Poetics* said about humour, but these are at best speculative. In any case, around 2,000 years later, Mel Brooks expressed succinctly the difference between comedy and tragedy: "Tragedy is when I cut my finger. Comedy is when you fall into an open sewer and die."

Even before Aristotle, however, comedy was treated with a good deal of seriousness by philosophers. Plato was highly suspicious of comedy and its capacity to induce laughter, which he saw as a loss of self-control. Around 375 BC he wrote in *The Republic*: "There is a principle in human nature which is disposed to raise a laugh, and this which you once restrained by reason, because you were afraid of being thought a buffoon, is now let out again; and having stimulated the risible faculty at the theatre, you are betrayed unconsciously to yourself into playing the comic poet at home."

Watching a tragedy enacted on stage, Plato argued, can be a valuable lesson in how to control our own negative emotions, but comedy is potentially destructive, especially in those entrusted with the guardianship of the state, and should be tightly controlled if self-control is to be preserved. He was particularly critical of excessive laughter which, he said, "always produces a violent reaction". Pursuing this theme, he singles out a passage in the *Iliad* in which Homer describes how "Inextinguishable laughter arose among the blessed gods". Plato argues: "Persons of worth, even if only mortal men, must not be represented as overcome by laughter, and still less must such a representation of the gods be allowed."

In Plato's moral treatise *Philebus*, he specifically identifies laughing at the ridiculous antics of others as "a certain kind of evil, specifically a vice". We are taking delight in the self-ignorance of others, which he says is morally objectionable.

Summing up his arguments against comedy in his last and longest work, *Laws*, Plato envisages an ideal state in which comedy is tightly controlled. A citizen should resist acting out any scene of ridiculousness but "we shall enjoin that such representations be left to slaves or hired aliens, and that they receive no serious consideration whatsoever. No free person, whether woman or man, shall be found taking lessons in them." Perhaps most damning of all, he says: "older children will be advocates of comedy; educated women, and young men, and people in general, will favour tragedy." In other words, comedy is not something for grown-ups.

This suspicious attitude toward comedy persisted until at least the 16th century and even after then was slow to fade. One might say that humourlessness among the guardians of the state has remained the norm until the present day.

With both Plato and Aristotle holding somewhat negative views about humour and laughter, it is hardly surprising that other Greek philosophers shared their reservations. The Stoic philosopher Epictetus, for example, who was born a slave around AD 50, advised: "Let not your laughter be loud, frequent, or unrestrained." According to his followers, he never laughed at all but he did have at least one fairly humorous line to his credit: "He who laughs at himself never runs out of things to laugh at."

By contrast, the philosopher Democritus, who was born around 460 BC and lived until he was 90, was known as "the laughing philosopher" for the great delight he took in ridiculing human follies. His views on the composition of the Milky Way and the atomic structure of matter were centuries ahead of their time, for which he had also been called "the father of modern science". It was probably his laughter rather than his science that caused him, according to some accounts, to be intensely despised by Plato, who thought that all of his books should be burned.

Despite several references to Democritus as a laughing philosopher, we are still rather unclear about what he was laughing at, though a hint is provided by a tale written around 200 years after his death, of a meeting with Hippocrates (of 'Hippocratic oath' fame). The story goes that Hippocrates, as the greatest medic of his time, is commissioned by Democritus's colleagues to cure him of the madness that made him laugh so much. After examining him, however, Hippocrates decides that Democritus is a truly wise man for being the only one among his so-called friends to understand the absurdity of human existence and laugh at it.

Moving on from the not-very-funny comedies of the ancient Greeks, the historical development of humour continued in ancient Rome where the oldest known book of jokes appeared in the third or fourth century AD. Under the title *Philogelos* (meaning "Lover of Laughter") it was written in Greek and consisted of around 260 jokes, some of which have been described as being similar to today's jokes. It is difficult to agree with that, unless one is in the habit of telling jokes about eunuchs or hernias or, presumably best of all, eunuchs with hernias. Apparently, philosophers were also a common target of jokes: "A philosopher stood before a mirror with his eyes shut, to see how handsome he was when he was asleep."

Stupid philosophers, however, were heavily outnumbered by stupid pedants: "A certain person meeting a pedant said, 'The slave you sold me died.' 'By the gods,' replied the other, 'he never did such a thing when he was with me.'"

By modern standards, perhaps the best joke in the collection was this: "A witty fellow being asked by a chattering barber, 'How shall I cut it?' replied, 'In silence.'" Over-talkative barbers have clearly been around for a very long time. As the esteemed classicist Mary Beard has pointed out, the witty fellow's response is exactly the same as the line delivered to the House of Commons barber by Enoch Powell in reply to the same question. As a professor of Greek before he entered politics, Powell was probably aware of the long pedigree of his joke.

The very existence of an ancient Roman book of jokes suggests that ordinary citizens at the time may not have been as keen to take quite such a negative view of humour as their philosophers thought appropriate. For many centuries, however, generations of philosophers tended to follow the Platonic suspicion of laughter. The following comments are typical:

> Seeing that it is a greater perfection to know the truth than to be ignorant of it, even when it is to our disadvantage, I must conclude that it is better to be less cheerful and possess more knowledge. So it is not always the most cheerful person who has the most satisfied mind; on the contrary great joys are commonly sober and serious, and only slight and passing joys are accompanied by laughter.
>
> René Descartes, in a letter to Princess
> Elisabeth of Bohemia, 1645

> When we think of the good or evil of other people, we may judge them worthy or unworthy of it. When we judge them worthy of it, that arouses in us solely the passion of joy, in so far as we get some benefit from seeing things happen as they ought; and the joy aroused in the case of a good differs from that aroused in the case of an evil only in that the former is serious whereas the latter is accompanied by laughter and derision.
>
> René Descartes, *The Passions of the Soul*, 1650

This deeply rooted suspicion of laughter reached its high point – or sank to its nadir, depending on one's point of view – in an extraordinary book published in 1875. *The Philosophy of Laughter and Smiling* by George Vasey is 166 pages long, comprising a closely argued diatribe directed against humour and laughter. Joke-writers, comedians and anyone who dares laugh at them all attract Vasey's scorn and particular venom is devoted to decrying the pernicious act of tickling babies. Typically, Chapter XV bears the title "On the degrading and vicious consequences of the habit of laughing" and begins with the following condemnation:

> In the present chapter we shall endeavour to point out that the obstreperous and meaningless habit of laughing is, if not the entire cause, at least one of the principal causes, of the existence and continuance of the follies, frivolities, mischiefs and low conversations which are now so rampant in every class of society, and which sink it so low in the moral scale.

Early in the book, he states that laughing is "a striking characteristic of idiotcy [sic]" and that "Sensible people – as may be observed every day – seldom laugh." He reserves particular criticism for "those highly-gifted individuals who have acquired the happy knack of writing, or mouthing and spouting, those facetious words, or of performing those grotesque actions, which have the magical power of contracting our cheeks into wrinkles, and distending our jugular veins", and makes it very clear that such people ought not to be encouraged: "The inhabitants of London alone spend many thousands of pounds annually to support in ease and elegance those dexterous and ingenious eccentrics whose only business it is to make their auditors or spectators laugh."

He rubs it in by pointing out that: "*In former times* to keep *one* fool to provoke laughter was considered so choice a luxury as only to be indulged in by a king. *At the present time* the common people can afford to keep some *hundreds*."

As for tickling babies, he argues that: "It is very questionable that children would ever begin to laugh if they were not stimulated or prompted, but were let alone, and treated naturally and rationally."

Moving on from the terrible effects of tickling babies to the damage inflicted on older children, he devotes Chapter XVI to "the injurious effects of nursery rhymes and juvenile literature in stultifying the minds of children and youths by furnishing them with extravagant lies and egregious nonsense to excite their wonder and induce them to laugh".

Getting into his stride, Vasey asks: "What are the words and actions which excite laughter? Are they not the absurd, the ridiculous, the mischievous, the sicked the lewd, the profane? Are they not words and actions that give pain to others?" And he goes on to say: "In the mildest of terms that can be applied to them, they are simply ridiculous and absurd, and certainly indicate a partial suspension of intellect or judgement, an emptiness of mind verging on imbecility."

In conclusion, he points out that: "Rationality, good sense, wisdom, virtue, righteousness are never laughed at", and sums up by saying: "we may very safely conclude that the universal predominance of these qualities would be the total annihilation of laughter."

The Greeks, as one would expect, had a word for followers of the Vasey creed: ἀγέλαστος meant "not laughing" and came into English in the 17th century as the term "agelastick" or later simply "agelast". In fact, the Greeks had another related word too: μισόγελως (hating laughter). That came into English as "misogelastic" in an article by George Meredith in 1877. This was just two years after the great laughter-hater George Vasey published his treatise. I suspect the two events may have been connected.

Vasey was a long way from being alone among Victorian Britons, who were distinctly suspicious of laughter. A less extreme but perhaps even more moralistic critic of laughter was the Reverend William Henry Lyttelton, rector of Hagley in Worcestershire and later canon of Gloucester Cathedral, whose writings on Christian theological matters included an essay over

7,250 words long on laughter in the *Good Words* magazine in 1869. It begins in characteristically pompous style:

> Notwithstanding the troublous character of the times
> (and what times are not troublous in this great battle-
> field of mighty evil and mightier good – this world?), and
> the many critical questions of vital importance which are
> occupying the minds of men, I scarcely think it needful
> to apologize for selecting for somewhat careful treatment
> the above subject, to the consideration of which
> circumstances have led me.

He then spends around 300 more words explaining why he didn't need to apologize, before launching his long-winded explanation of when laughter is permissible, when it is sinful, and who can be trusted to laugh.

Lyttelton reserves his greatest invective for those who laugh in church:

> As to wantonly laughing in sacred places – as in the
> midst of a congregation gathered for Divine worship – it
> is the sin of poor, of shallow, of unworthy, or of over-
> youthful souls. The sight of a wanton boy, or a silly
> wench, or of men and women who have not outgrown
> their childishness, wilfully laughing in church, suggests
> the thought of a monkey who, in illicit ways, should have
> climbed the walls of Heaven, and intruded his ignoble
> chatter and soulless sport among the august Presences
> THERE. And it should receive the treatment which that
> would merit – the expulsion of the offender with sharp
> decisiveness, and a deserved ignominy. If in jesting you
> are led into dancing over the lines of the Divine morality,
> and of Divine reverence, and so fall down some precipices
> of the Divine vengeance, or lead others to that result,
> it will be poor comfort to reflect that you were dancing
> when you did so.

He also condemns "impure jests" and "wanton jests", and registers a strong protest against "making drunkenness a subject for laughter, at least in mixed company".

The main trouble with Lyttelton's rules for determining, in any given circumstances, whether laughter is morally permissible and if so, by whom, is that they are so detailed, meticulously laid out and constantly tripping over their own convoluted arguments that by the time anyone has worked out whether it is okay to laugh, they will have forgotten what they were thinking of laughing at in the first place.

Finally, we should go back to the quotation with which we started this chapter: "A serious and good philosophical work could be written that would consist entirely of jokes." This comes from *Ludwig Wittgenstein: A Memoir* by his pupil, friend and colleague Norman Malcolm, who sadly does not expand on the statement. Wittgenstein himself, however, ended the introduction to his *Philosophical Investigations* with these words: "I should have liked to produce a good book. This has not come about, but the time is past in which I could improve it." Sadly, he died in 1951 before completing that work, but perhaps we should be grateful that he never wrote what by his standards might have been "a serious and good philosophical work". As I hope this chapter has made abundantly clear, anything written by philosophers or theologians on the subject of jokes is liable to be tedious, over-long, and not at all funny.

So let's finish with three short jokes that were all voted Best Joke at the Edinburgh Fringe in recent years. Their themes show that thanks to developments in language and technology, there will always be new opportunities to be funny: the theme of these three are soccer, vacuum cleaners and passwords:

The 2015 winner for Tommy Tiernan: "Two flies are playing football in a saucer. One says to the other: 'Make an effort, we're playing in the cup tomorrow.'"

The 2014 winner for Tim Vine: "I've decided to sell my Hoover … well, it was just collecting dust."

And my favourite, by Nick Helm in 2011: "I needed a password eight characters long so I picked Snow White and the Seven Dwarfs."

2

DO GODS LAUGH?

"I said of laughter, It is mad: and of mirth, What doeth it?"

Ecclesiastes, 2:2

As we have seen, philosophers, following the arguments of Plato and, to a lesser extent Aristotle, have always had a hard time dealing with humour, but their problems have been small compared with the tangle theologians – especially Christian theologians – have found themselves in for at least the last 500 years. So let's start with an inoffensively funny, if excruciatingly punny, theological joke:

> After the successful disembarkment of the Ark on Mount Ararat, God told Noah to build another boat. "Same as last time?" asked Noah. "Animals two by two again?"
>
> "You forgot the fish last time," God said, "so we'll need a bigger ark with more decks on different levels. And I don't want just any fish. I particularly want carp."
>
> "Right," said Noah: "You want a multi-storey carp ark."

Back to the philosophical humorous tangle facing philosophers, the cause is simple: God created man in his own image; laughter is a feature of mankind; God must therefore laugh; but laughter at best involves a loss of control and at worst can be thoroughly nasty.

Various ways around this dilemma have been suggested, including a suggestion that only God is capable of true, unsullied laughter; or the idea that we humans won't know the real wonder of laughter until we get to heaven; or the suggestion that God is indeed capable of laughter, but has sufficient godly restraint not to do it. Another of the problems this all raises, however, is that most laughter is a reaction to some sort of surprise or something unexpected, but how can either of those happen to an omniscient deity?

Looking for answers in the Bible does not help much either. Proverbs 17:22 may tell us that "A merry heart doeth good like a medicine: but a broken spirit drieth the bones", but Proverbs 14:13 says: "Even in laughter the heart is sorrowful; and the end of that mirth is heaviness", and Ecclesiastes 7:3 casts another vote against laughter by saying: "Sorrow is better than laughter: for by the sadness of the countenance the heart is made better." Indeed, in the King James Bible (1611) the word "slaughter" occurs 56 times, while "laughter" scores only seven – and most of those are uncomplimentary.

Just look at the following tables of the ten most joyous and miserable words in the Old and New Testaments of the Bible:

Happy	OT	NT	Sad	OT	NT
Love	124	156	Fear	307	78
Joy	95	60	Anger	223	5
Loved	51	38	Cry	159	9
Kindness	37	6	Wrath	149	45
Loveth	34	23	Cried	129	66
Joyful	24	1	Desolate	125	7
Kind	23	9	Hate	69	16
Merry	21	7	Wept	55	13
Happy	19	6	Feared	53	19
Laugh	15	2	Sorrow	52	13

16

The words "laugh", "laughed", "laugheth", "laughing" and "laughter" between them occur 33 times in the Old Testament and six in the New, compared with totals of 118 plus 43 for "weep", "weepest", "weepeth", "weeping" and "wept", while "cry", "cries", "criest", "cried", "crieth" and "crying" together score an impressive 318 in the Old Testament and 99 in the New.

This may seem partially counterbalanced by a score of 184 for "joy", "joyous" and "joyful", until you notice that "anger" and "angry" score 271, while "desolate" and "desolation" rack up 178. Perhaps all this is what Luke 6:25 is warning us of when he says: "Woe unto you that laugh now", while James 4:9 advises us: "Be afflicted, and mourn, and weep: let your laughter be turned to mourning, and your joy to heaviness."

Taking into account the fact that the Old Testament contains more than three times as many words as the New, it is interesting to note that the most marked differences between them are the high levels of fear, anger and desolation in the Old and the increased amount of love and joy in the New.

Neither scores well on laughter, perhaps because laughing got off to a bad and confusing start in the Bible with the story of Abraham and Sarah, as recounted in Chapters 17 and 18 of the Book of Genesis. It all starts with God telling Abraham that he will be the "father of many nations" and laying down the rules he must obey. To fulfil this, God says he will give Sarah a son, which Abraham finds very amusing, as Genesis 17:17 tells us: "Then Abraham fell upon his face, and laughed, and said in his heart, Shall a child be born unto him that is an hundred years old? and shall Sarah, that is ninety years old, bear?"

God confirms that is indeed what will happen: "And God said, Sarah thy wife shall bear thee a son indeed; and thou shalt call his name Isaac" (Genesis 17:19). That name reflects Abraham's response as "Isaac" is a version of the Hebrew name "Yitzhak", which means "laughter".

That seems to confirm that God has a sense of humour, but the following chapter tells us what happens when Sarah hears the news from God. The apparent problem in God's plan is confirmed in Genesis 18:11: "Abraham and Sarah were old and well stricken in age; and it ceased to be with Sarah after the manner of women", which explains Sarah's reaction to it and God's perhaps surprising response:

> Therefore Sarah laughed within herself, saying, After I am waxed old shall I have pleasure, my lord being old also?
> And the Lord said unto Abraham, Wherefore did Sarah laugh, saying, Shall I of a surety bear a child, which am old? Is any thing too hard for the Lord? At the time appointed I will return unto thee, according to the time of life, and Sarah shall have a son.
> Then Sarah denied, saying, I laughed not; for she was afraid. And he said, Nay; but thou didst laugh.
>
> Genesis 18:12–15

So basically what happened is that when God told the 99-year-old Abraham and 90-year-old Sarah they were going to have a baby, Abraham fell about laughing and Sarah wondered whether she would enjoy the experience, then laughed and said: "You must be joking", in reply to which God said, "I never joke, and you shouldn't have laughed." Sarah got scared and denied laughing and God, being omniscient, told her she was fibbing.

Actually, the short account in Genesis adds to the complexity by pointing out that Sarah did not receive the news directly from God but overheard his conversation with Abraham and two men who were really angels in disguise. The question has therefore been raised of whether God was rebuking Sarah not for laughing but for eavesdropping or possibly for laughing at a joke that she was not intended to hear anyway.

So what was going on? Why does God apparently rebuke Sarah for laughing, while seeming to reward Abraham for the same reaction by telling him to give their son a name meaning "laughter"?

There are several reasons to be uncertain about biblical references to laughter and one of them is the problem of translation. Most of the Old Testament was originally written in Hebrew and most of the New Testament was in Greek, both of which languages had two main verbs that can be translated as "laugh". There is some argument about the precise difference between these verbs, but in both languages, one was generally used for natural and joyous laughter, happy and unbridled, while the other was a more malicious laughter, deriding or making fun of someone or something. There is also the question of the use of different prepositions with the verbs of laughter: laughing *at* someone can be very different from laughing *with* them, but analyses of the usage of all these verbs and prepositions in both Old and New Testaments does not yield the consistent results one would hope for.

In addition, there is the little matter of confirmation bias among the people performing such analyses. As many psychological experiments have shown, when even the best-trained scientists are testing a hypothesis, they have a natural tendency to perform experiments and collect results and observations that confirm their hypothesis rather than those that challenge it. Theologians who want to find humour in the scriptures will have no difficult in citing passages they see as examples of it, just as anyone seeking godly humourlessness will have no problem finding examples of that.

As the impressionist and comedian Rory Bremner once said: "I think if there is a God, it's very important that he has a sense of humour – otherwise, you are in for a very miserable afterlife." Anyone searching the Bible for confirmation of this desirable state is therefore likely to suffer from confirmation bias, making them eager to support the hypothesis of a laughing God.

In 2014, Professor Hennie A. J. Kruger of the School of Religion, Philosophy and Classics at the University of KwaZulu-Natal, South Africa wrote an intriguing paper with the title "Laughter in the Old Testament: A hotchpotch of humour, mockery and rejoicing?" He begins by stating, "It would appear that many people who read the Bible take the view that it accommodates humour", and then asks: "but what is the factual situation?" He then proceeds to analyse all the instances of laughter in the Old Testament, giving particular attention to the precise meaning of the original Hebrew. His conclusion does not hold out great prospects for Rory Bremner's afterlife: "This article does not augur well for the conviction that the Old Testament contains material of a humorous character."

The same theme forms an important part of Umberto Eco's extraordinary novel *The Name of the Rose* in which the erudite but evil monk Jorge has found the lost second volume of Aristotle's *Poetics* hidden in the monastery library. This volume sees the great philosopher's positive views on the merits of humour and laughter, which Jorge considers a "perfidious theology" and dedicates himself to ensuring that Aristotle's message is not discovered or spread, even if he has to kill anyone who finds the book. He cannot, of course, just burn the book, because that would be a sin far greater than merely murdering people.

Such negative views of humour by religious killjoys and killjokes dominated Protestant ideology in the Middle Ages. *The Name of the Rose* is set in 14th-century Italy, which was a century and a half before the start of the Spanish Inquisition, after which another century passed before Puritanism gained power in England, but they all shared a similar suspicion of laughter and other forms of gratuitous pleasure.

The natural question to ask is whether this suspicion of humour is peculiar to Christianity or whether other religions exhibit similar prejudice. An attempt to investigate that question was reported in the *European Journal of Humour Research* in 2018 under the title "Does religion shape people's sense of humour?: A comparative study of humour appreciation among members of different religions and non-believers". The research took the form of a questionnaire comprising 24 jokes or cartoons that subjects were asked to rate for funniness and offensiveness. Eighteen of the jokes had religious themes, but six were non-religious to allow comparisons to be made.

Respondents were also asked their age, sex, religion and whether they were practising believers, and what region of the world they came from. There were not enough Jews, Mormons or Buddhists among the respondents, so these were classified as 'Other' and added to the control group with which respondents were compared. There were also two groups who identified themselves as 'Atheist' or 'Agnostic'.

After eliminating responses for various reasons, which included many subjects who said they did not understand the jokes, the researchers were left with large enough samples of Christian, Islam, Hindu, Atheist and Agnostic respondents to analyse the differences between them, including how they reacted to religious jokes compared with non-religious, and how they reacted to jokes about their own religion compared with those targeting other religions.

The demographic information indicated great disparity between the countries of origin of the different groups: 89 per cent of the Christians, 97 per cent of the Agnostics and 87 per cent of the Atheists came from the USA, while 97 per cent of the Hindu sample were from India. The Islamic sample was more equally spread with 50 per cent American and 41 per cent Indian respondents, but those figures must raise the possibility that any differences between the groups may be due to national culture rather than religion.

Among their findings, the researchers reported that "we did find that religious self-classification had a measurable and statistically significant impact on the quality of humour appreciation" and "Muslims' humour appreciation exceeded that of other groups", while Christians gave the lowest humour ratings.

All groups, however, agreed on which the funniest and least funny items were. The least funny was an anti-Christian cartoon from the magazine *Charlie Hebdo* depicting the Father, the Son and the Holy Ghost engaging in a sex act, which scored an average of 2.9 on the nine-point humour scale, while the funniest, scoring 6.7, was this non-religious joke:

A man kills a deer and takes it home to cook for dinner. Both he and his wife decide that they won't tell the kids what kind of meat it is, but will give them a clue and let them guess. The dad said, "Well, it's what Mommy calls me sometimes." The little girl screamed to her brother, "Don't eat it! It's an asshole!"

3
NO LAUGHING MATTER

"Comedy is about envy, greed, malice, avarice, lust, stupidity."
John Cleese on *The Dick Cavett Show*
on PBS in America in 1979

Philosophers had a problem with humour for more than two thousand years. As the first chapter of this book explained, this was largely due to the influence of Plato and his followers, whose attitude toward laughter ranged from suspicion to outright hostility. To understand this better, we need to make a foray into the history of language, but first, let's have an awful quadruple pun that includes a philosopher:

Q: Why is it illogical to have to choose between a Russian tyrant, a French philosopher, fillet steak or a brothel?
A: It's Putin, Descartes, beef or the whores.

As we have already mentioned, the words "humour" and "comedy" had meanings that were very different from their later usage. Nowadays, people almost universally approve of what we call a "sense of humour", yet the earliest recorded citation for that phrase in the *Oxford English Dictionary* was in 1753, which was more than 400 years after the word "humour" had entered the language for a supposed bodily fluid. Interestingly, the term "humour blindness" was applied in 1798 not, as anyone today might assume, to describe someone who cannot understand a joke, but as a term for an optical ailment in horses.

It was not so much humour (in its modern sense) that infuriated Plato as the laughter that it might cause, and the early writers on the subject seemed to have problems separating the idea of laughing *at* someone with the idea of laughing *with* them. Laughter itself was seen as a potentially malicious expression of scorn and benevolent laughter was treated with the same philosophical ignominy.

Attempts to apply philosophy to humour, however, have always run into the same problem: philosophy, which came from two Greek words meaning "lover of wisdom", seeks to explain the world; humour generally results from a distortion of the world. The two simply do not fit together comfortably, as we shall see in the survey of theories of humour that follows. Philosophers and comedians are two very different species.

The Superiority Theory

This was the theory that dominated philosophical writings about humour from the ancient Greeks until the 18th century, though it was not referred to by that name until the 20th century when other theories began to be advanced to replace or at least augment it.

Plato originally laid out his argument in his Socratic dialogue *Philebus* in a notional conversation between Socrates and Protarchus. Socrates points out that when seeing a comedy "the soul experiences a mixture of pain and pleasure", going on to explain that "the malicious man is somehow pleased at his neighbour's misfortunes." After a long exploration of the evil of malice, he concludes: "When we laugh at what is ridiculous in our friends, our pleasure, in mixing with malice, mixes with pain, for we have agreed that malice is a pain of the soul, and that laughter is pleasant, and on these occasions we both feel malice and laugh."

Aristotle was a little less harsh about comedy, describing the ludicrous in his *Rhetoric* as "a failing or a piece of ugliness which causes no pain or destruction" and wit as "educated insolence".

The ancient Greeks, however, fell short of creating an all-embracing theory of humour, but contented themselves with explaining what was wrong with it.

The beginnings of a proper theory had to wait until 1651, when the English philosopher Thomas Hobbes published *Leviathan*, covering all aspects of the structure of society and government. Perceiving people as naturally individualistic and competitive, he saw winning and losing as important to us, creating good and bad feelings respectively. "Sudden glory", he wrote, "is the passion which makes those grimaces called laughter; and is caused either by some sudden act of their own, that pleases them; or by the apprehension of some deformed thing in another, by comparison whereof they suddenly applaud themselves." Developing this theme, Hobbes explained that: "the passion of laughter is nothing else but sudden glory arising from some sudden conception of some eminency in ourselves, by comparison with the infirmity of others, or with our own formerly." In other words, a feeling of one's own superiority, or the failings of others, is a basic component of humour. And he went on to say that "it is incident most to them, that are conscious of the fewest abilities in themselves; who are forced to keep themselves in their own favour, by observing the imperfections of other men. And therefore much Laughter at the defects of others is a signe of Pusillanimity."

This may be of great use in rationalizing the condemnation of certain types of humour, such as malicious sneering or laughing at someone else's expense, but Superiority Theory is clearly inadequate in explaining why a vast number of situations are considered funny by many people. Unlike Plato, Aristotle and Hobbes, let's see what happens when we test this and other Theories of Humour on a sample set of ten jokes:

J1: we have encountered before this one before: "A dyslexic walked into a bra."

J2: was found in a 2002 study of jokes to be the funniest of all those included: "Two hunters went out into the wilderness together and one of them suddenly collapsed and died. The other, in a panic, phoned the emergency services. 'Calm down,' he was told. 'The first thing we must do is make sure he is dead.' The caller then left the phone and a gunshot was heard. 'Right, done that,' the caller said when he returned to the phone. 'What comes next?'"

The other jokes in our sample are, you will be pleased to hear, shorter ...

J3: A patient entered a surgery and told the doctor he had a strawberry stuck up his bum. "I have some cream for that," the doctor said.

J4: Two ducks were in a pond. One of them said: "Quack." The other replied: "I was just about to say that."

J5: There was a young man from Peru, Whose limerick stopped at line two.

J6: Two fish are in a tank. One says to the other, "Do you know how to drive this?"

J7: Why did the chicken go to the séance? To get to the other side.

J8: Helvetica and Times New Roman walk into a bar. "Get out!" shouts the barman. "We don't serve your types."

J9: A sloth is crawling along a road when he is set upon and beaten up by a gang of snails who leave him injured and bloody in the street and go off laughing. When the sloth has recovered a little, he drags himself to a police station to report the assault. "Did you get a good look at your assailants?" the policemen asks. "Can you give us a description of them?" And the sloth says, "It all happened so fast."

J10: A farmer asked me to help him round up his 47 sheep. I said, "50."

So how does the Superiority Theory score on each of these jokes:

J1: I suppose one might consider a dyslexic one's literary inferior, or feel superior to anyone walking into a bra, but that's not why the joke is funny.

J2: This one does better: the humour inherent in stupidity-based misunderstanding may be attributed to a feeling of superiority.

J3: I suppose not having a strawberry stuck up one's bum is superior to having one there, but the joke is in the cream not the strawberry.

J4: You could say we have clear linguistic superiority over an animal that can only say "Quack", but that's not the point.

J5: Is a normal five-line limerick superior to this two-line limerick? I think not.

J6: The humour is entirely in the double meaning of "tank". No superiority involved.

J7: You could say that the joke-teller feels superiority when revealing that the riddle has the same answer as the original "why did the chicken cross the road" joke, but the main humour comes from the double meaning of "other side".

J8: Surely people are not affected by considering themselves superior to typefaces?

J9: In my experience this always evoked sympathy for sloths rather than a feeling of superiority.

J10: Another misunderstanding, based on the double meaning of "round up". I suppose one could feel superior to the joke-teller for not knowing what the farmer meant by "round up".

We see from all this that the Superiority Theory does not do very well in explaining the humour in these jokes, but it fails on another level too. Even if superiority or inadequacy were an essential feature of jokes, a proper theory would need to account for those situations in which superiority/inadequacy exists but humour is not a consequence. A sudden realization of superiority may just as easily result in pity, or compassion, or sadness. What is the missing ingredient that makes it funny?

Before passing judgement on the ancient philosophers, however, we should remember that Plato and Aristotle lived more than two millennia ago and Hobbes more than two centuries before Karl Popper added rigour to the philosophy of science with his criterion of "falsifiability" to judge whether a hypothesis is even worth considering. Popper's essential point was that a scientific theory must make testable predictions which would show that the theory is wrong if they are not confirmed.

The Greeks provided a fine example of pre-falsifiability illogic as Bertrand Russell pointed out in his 1943 essay *An Outline of Intellectual Rubbish*: "Aristotle could have avoided the mistake of thinking that women have fewer teeth than men, by the simple device of asking Mrs Aristotle to keep her mouth open while he counted." Aristotle, however, was not interested in potential falsification of the theories that led him to believe that men's and women's tooth numbers were bound to be different, so he preferred that Mrs Aristotle kept her mouth shut.

Perhaps the fact that we can laugh at that now is because it makes us feel superior to Aristotle, which shows that Superiority Theory still has its uses, but other humour theories are clearly also required.

The Relief Theory

During the 18th and 19th centuries, a new theory slowly developed that stemmed from considering the physical process of laughing. Just as Plato had disapproved of laughter because it showed loss of control, the new interpretation was that it represented a benign and useful release of tension.

Perhaps the first to suggest this explanation was Anthony Ashley-Cooper, 3rd Earl of Shaftesbury, in his 1709 "Essay on the Freedom of Wit and Humour", which, incidentally, was one of the first works to use the word "humour" in its modern sense. His explanation of laughter, however, owed a great deal to the older idea of humours as almost mystical bodily fluids. He wrote:

> The natural free spirits of ingenious men, if imprisoned or controlled, will find out other ways of motion to relieve themselves in their constraint; and whether it be in burlesque, mimicry, or buffoonery, they will be glad at any rate to vent themselves, and be revenged upon their constrainers.

In other words, laughter is a pressure-release mechanism, providing relief from built-up stresses. This idea was developed in the 19th century by two highly influential philosophers.

Herbert Spencer (1820–1903) was one of the major intellectual figures of his time and was even the man who, after reading Darwin's *Origin of Species*, coined the phrase "survival of the fittest" and extended evolutionary principles to the development of social structures. In 1860, he also wrote *The Physiology of Laughter*, which developed Shaftesbury's ideas into a "hydraulic" theory involving a build-up of nervous energy of excitement and agitation which, he said, "must expend itself in some way or other". This was his explanation of apparently purposeless laughter.

That idea was developed by an even more famous (and, incidentally, even more humourless) thinker, in 1905, which was when Sigmund Freud wrote his *Jokes and Their Relation to the Unconscious*, which must be the least funny book ever with the word "jokes" in its title. We shall return to Freud's *Jokes* later, but all we need to know at the moment is how he developed Relief Theory.

Freud goes into more detail than Spencer about the nature of laughter, dividing its sources into jokes, the comic and plain humour, explaining in each case how energy is built up before being dissipated in laughter. In jokes, the energy comes from repressed sexual feelings and hostility; in the comic, it is cognitive energy that builds up; in humour it is emotional energy. But Freud never tells us what form these energies take nor where and how they are stored.

Perhaps the main objection to the Relief Theory, however, comes from the idea of laughter being caused by built-up tension. This would suggest that the people who laugh the most and the longest are the most nervous, twitchiest, repressed and worrying members of society, yet our experience suggests the exact opposite.

Looking at our sample of ten jokes reveals some of the strengths and weaknesses of the Relief Theory:

J1   is interesting: in the joke itself, there is no build-up of tension, but Freud's cognitive energy builds in the listener's mind after the end of the joke when working out what is going on. First, there is the surprise of the early ending when most walks-into-a-bar jokes continue for some time, and second, the listener needs a moment to work out why the dyslexic walked into a bra. Whether this takes long enough to lead to an explosion of mirth, however, is rather doubtful.

J2   also needs time for the listener to work out what happened, though the shot ringing out is a big clue.

J3:   I doubt that the cream will bring much relief.

J4:   The only relief I can see here comes from the realization that the scenario is complete nonsense.

J5:   This is a good example of the relief of puzzle-solving: the listener expects the limerick to go on but must work out why it stopped at line two. This takes time and there are always some seconds between hearing this joke and resulting laughter.

J6:   There is a triple level of relief here: first on encountering talking goldfish, then on the question of whether goldfish can drive, and finally the realization that they are in a military vehicle. There is a lot of tension to resolve here.

I have come across one laborious explanation of this joke given by someone who completely misses the point that it is not a fish tank they are in.

J7: All riddles are good examples of Relief Theory: they offer the relief of finding or hearing the solution to a puzzle.

J8: This involves relief on noticing the double meaning of "type".

J9: I see no true relief here: it is the entire scenario that is funny, accentuated by the sloth's final response.

J10: Like many jokes, this one relies on setting up an expectation in the listener's mind, then diverting it. That is a nice way of building up tension then releasing it dramatically. We shall have more to say about that technique when we come to Arthur Koestler's Bisociation Theory later in this chapter.

Incongruity Theory

As Superiority Theory became increasingly to be seen as existing at best behind certain types of humour and Relief Theory was doing better but failed really to explain itself, an alternative began to attract many philosophical heavyweights. Immanuel Kant, Arthur Schopenhauer and Søren Kierkegaard all made attempts to explain humour through versions of Incongruity Theory, though the idea behind it dates back far longer. Cicero's long essay *De Oratore* ("On The Orator"), written around 55 BC, contains a long section on wit and humour in which he says: "what excites laughter is disappointing expectations", which is as brief and precise a summary of Incongruity Theory as one could wish for.

The task of turning Incongruity into a formal Theory, however, was begun by the Scottish poet and philosopher James Beattie (1735–1803) in *An Essay on Laughter, and Ludicrous Composition* published in 1779. In general, Beattie was a very minor figure in philosophy, but his views on humour were spot on. He began his essay with the words: "Of man, it is observed by Homer, that he is the most wretched, and, by Addison and others, that he is the merriest animal in the whole creation: and both opinions are plausible, and both perhaps may be true."

Beattie went on to assert that: "Laughter arises from the view of two or more inconsistent, unsuitable, or incongruous parts or circumstances, considered as united in one complex object or assemblage, or as acquiring a sort of mutual reaction from the peculiar manner in which the mind takes notice of them."

This was perhaps the first time the word "incongruous" had been advanced as an explanation of laughter and its attraction was clear. Almost all common causes of laughter had something incongruous about them, from tickling, which is a benign form of an apparently aggressive act, to any joke with a build-up that is derailed by a surprise punchline.

Even the notoriously solemn and usually depressed Arthur Schopenhauer was convinced by the idea, though he was definitely not the world's greatest stand-up comic, as his explanation of one of his favourite jokes attests. The joke that attracted him so much consisted basically of asking what the angle is between a circle and its tangent. This, apparently, never failed to have him rolling in the aisles, though the explanation he gives in *The World as Will and Idea* (*Die Welt als Wille und Vorstellung*, 1818) leaves much to be desired:

> If we consider that an angle requires two lines meeting
> so that if they are produced they will intersect each
> other; on the other hand, that the tangent of a circle
> only touches it at one point, but at this point is really
> parallel to it; and accordingly have present to our minds
> the abstract conviction of the impossibility of an angle
> between the circumference of a circle and its tangent; and
> if now such an angle lies visibly before us upon paper,
> this will easily excite a smile. The ludicrousness in this
> case is exceedingly weak; but yet the source of it in the

incongruity of what is thought and perceived appears in it with exceptional distinctness. When we discover such an incongruity, the occasion for laughter that thereby arises is, according as we pass from the real, i.e., the perceptible, to the conception, or conversely from the conception to the real, either a witticism or an absurdity, which in a higher degree, and especially in the practical sphere, is folly.

Thank you, Herr Schopenhauer. Don't call us; we'll call you.

The above explanation does, however, illustrate the main problem with Incongruity Theory. Even if sources of jokes and other humour always feature some type of incongruity, there are plenty of cases of incongruity that are not funny. Schopenhauer's extremely convoluted identification of incongruity in a matter of geometry may have convinced him that the very idea behind it is funny, but even if we accept the incongruity, we may not share his mirth.

Returning to our control sample of ten jokes, however, we do find considerable evidence of incongruity:

J1 features the incongruity of a dyslexic walking into a misspelling; in **J2**, it is the stupidity of the surviving hunter that is unexpected; in **J3** it is the alternative possibilities of treating strawberries with cream.

In **J4**, a talking duck is enough to confound expectations; **J5** has the obvious incongruity between the two-line limerick and the expected five lines; while **J6** subverts expectations concerning fish and tanks.

J7, J8 and J10, as we have already pointed out, create expectations and then subvert them, while the poor sloth in **J9** created an impression in our minds that he is behaving in a human-like manner, but then reverts to his usual slow sloth speed in the last line. This application of incongruity is a clever and funny switchback.

Although explaining some aspects of humour, the unsatisfactory elements of the Superiority, Relief and Incongruity theories led to various modifications, of which three in particular are worth mentioning.

Mechanical Humour

The highly influential French philosopher Henri Bergson found the theories discussed above unconvincing, largely for the reasons outlined, but in his 1900 work *Le Rire* (which was translated as *Laughter, An Essay on the Meaning of the Comic*) he came up with another theory that was equally incomplete.

Bergson's approach, however, changed the direction of humour research by changing attitudes toward laughter itself. Philosophers from Plato onwards had concentrated on the negative aspects of laughter, stressing its malevolent aspects and the lack of control it exhibited, but Bergson wrote of laughter's social role. Pointing out that apes grin and respond well to tickling, he saw laughter in humans as a positive evolutionary development of traits that could bind people together and strengthen social bonds.

Bergson's model of humour saw it as a specific example of incongruity, caused by the conflict between normal human flexibility and mechanistic behaviour. A person slipping on a banana peel is funny because it changes that individual's normally controlled progress to something mechanical, changing the person from subject to object.

In his 1964 book *The Act of Creation*, however, Arthur Koestler pointed out severe limitations in Bergson's theory of Mechanistic Humour:

> If rigidity contrasted with organic suppleness were
> laughable in itself, Egyptian statues and Byzantine
> mosaics would be the best jokes ever invented. If

automatic repetitiveness in human behaviour were a necessary and sufficient condition of the comic there would be no more amusing spectacle than an epileptic fit; and if we wanted a good laugh we would merely have to feel a person's pulse or listen to his heart-beat, with its monotonous tick-tack.

Quoting a line from Bergson's book, Koestler ends with a brilliantly devastating line: "If we 'laugh each time a person gives us the impression of being a thing' there would be nothing more funny than a corpse." (p.48 of Koestler's book). He does, however, praise Bergson for one line which he says comes close to the essence of humour: "A situation is always comic if it participates simultaneously in two series of events which are absolutely independent of each other and if it can be interpreted in two quite different meanings." Partly inspired by that thought, Koestler came up with a humour theory for which he invented a new word: bisociation.

The insight that inspired *The Act of Creation* was Koestler's identification of a common process underlying scientific creativity, artistic creativity and humour. All three involve transcending usual logic by bringing together ideas that already exist to create something new. With jokes, the process usually involves creating one storyline in the mind of the listener while an alternative explanation is going on along a parallel line. The truth only become clear to the listener when the first storyline is derailed and jumps onto the other. The excellence of the joke, and the extent of our laughter, depend both on the extent of the final leap and the ease with which it is accomplished in the mind of the listener.

Koestler's bisociation can be seen as another way of expressing the idea behind Incongruity Theory that is particularly suited to explaining jokes, but another refinement of Incongruity has also gained popularity recently, which we will come to next.

Benign Violation Theory

Time for another joke, I think:

Q: Why did the monkey fall from the tree?
A: Because it was dead.

In the mid-1980s, the American linguist Thomas Veatch heard this joke and says that he laughed for about an hour, though he was not quite sure what made it so funny. This set him off on a long search for a theory of humour that would explain it and he eventually outlined his findings in 1998 in a paper entitled "A Theory of Humor" in *Humor: International Journal of Humor Research*.

He called his new theory N+V, in which the V stands for "Violation" and the N was "Normal", and the idea behind it was that humour results from a conflict between Normality and a Violation of some sort of moral code. In the case of the above joke, the dead monkey is a violation of acceptable norms for answers to a joke, despite the fact that it is perfectly normal for a dead monkey to fall from a tree – indeed, it is only to be expected. As he pointed out, however, sometimes the Normality is made funny by a Violating punch-line, but it may equally happen the other way round. In our J9 sloth joke, for example, the early lines are a violation of everything we know about sloths and snails, but the punchline "It all happened so fast" is a perfectly normal response to the policeman's question.

These insights, however, were largely ignored for several years until around 2010, when two academics from the University of Colorado, Peter McGraw and Caleb Warren, restored life to Veatch's dead monkey by making a small change. They kept the Violation part, but the contrast, instead of being characterized as "Normal" was called "Benign" and the Benign Violation Theory of Humour (BVT) was born.

The idea is that a Violation occurs when one's beliefs about the world are undermined or threatened – but it is only funny if the Violation is seen to be benign. More specifically, the proponents of BVT maintain that humour occurs only when three conditions apply:

1. A Violation (of moral codes or expectations, for example) occurs;
2. The situation is Benign;
3. Both the above conditions occur simultaneously.

At present, this is the closest we have yet come to a general theory of humour that accounts for some things being perceived as funny, while other things are seen as not funny.

So what are we to make of all these diverse theories? Is any of them right? Are all of them right, or are they mutually incompatible, and if so, to what extent? In 2011, Matthew Hurley, Daniel Dennett and Reginald B. Adams Jr came up not so much with a new all-embracing theory but a radically new way of looking at the problem. Their book *Inside Jokes,* which they subtitled "using humour to reverse engineer the mind", was based on Hurley's dissertation at Tufts University in Boston, where he was supervised by his two co-authors, the esteemed philosopher Dennett and social psychologist Adams. Although the book does not quite fulfil its promise of developing a new Theory of Humour, it gives a convincing outline of what such a theory might look like and how it can be achieved.

After discussing the limitations of the existing theories, they adopt an approach based on evolution. Humour, after all, like any other emotion in humans, has evolved, so the first question to ask concerns its survival value. What is it that has given those possessing humour genes an advantage? Seeing the point of a joke, they reason, is a form of problem-solving, and feeling a pleasurable emotion called mirth or laughter when doing so has evolved in a manner that has led to greater mental capacity and quicker recognition of danger. Humour, in short, has led to a very useful improvement in the way we think.

Toward the end of *Inside Jokes,* the authors remind us of the Indian fable concerning six blind men and an elephant. The first falls against the animal's side and comments on how like a wall it is; the second closely examines a tusk and concludes that the elephant is like a spear; and so it goes on, with the others finding its trunk, its knee, its ear and its tail, which provoke comments about its similarity to a snake, a tree, a fan and a rope.

The 19th-century American poet John Godfrey Saxe told this story in his celebrated rhyme "The Blind Men and the Elephant", ending thus:

And so these men of Indostan
Disputed loud and long,
Each in his own opinion
Exceeding stiff and strong,
Though each was partly in the right,
And all were in the wrong!

Hurley, Dennett and Adams quote this verse in the final chapter of their book, seeing an analogy with the manner in which different philosophers of the past have all examined a different aspect of humour and come up with a different theory. "All that is missing", they say, "is a way of unifying the various descriptions of the elephant – of joining the parts that each theorist has wrapped his hands around – to show that they all are right."

They could equally have quoted the moral Saxe gave to the story:

So, oft in theologic wars
The disputants, I ween,
Rail on in utter ignorance
Of what each other mean,
And prate about an Elephant
Not one of them has seen!

This ties in very well with what Hurley and Co say about the philosophers who preceded them: "Each has been wrong only in declaring itself an alternative to all the others." Whether their new evolutionary approach will succeed in yielding a Grand Unified Theory of Humour, however, has yet to be seen.

If their theorizing has not yet reached a conclusion, perhaps we should remember Stephen Wright's definition: "A conclusion is the place where you got tired of thinking", and that, I would suggest, is something philosophers will never tire of.

Before leaving the theory of jokes, let me conclude with a final comment on our J4 joke about ducks. In 2001, the British Science Association began a rather informal international study on jokes in which various jokes were suggested by individuals around the world to find out what people found funniest in different cultures. Early in the experiment, they received the following joke: "There were two cows in a field. One said: 'Moo.' The other one said: 'I was going to say that!'"

In approved scientific style, they tried comparing that joke with other versions in which the cows going "moo" were replaced by mice going "eek", cats going "miaow", dogs going "woof" and an assortment of other animals. In terms of funniest ratings, the original cows came only third, just behind cats, but the clear winners were ducks going "quack".

The psychologist Richard Wiseman attributed this ducky success to the inherent funniness of the K-sound, which several comedians have commented upon, including Krusty the Clown in *The Simpsons* who was once forced to visit a faith healer because he had paralysed his vocal cords by trying to cram too many Ks into his comedy routines.

Yet a far older mention of the comedic power of K came in Neil Simon's 1972 play *The Sunshine Boys* in which an ageing comedian gives his nephew a lesson about funny words: "You know what words are funny and which words are not funny. Alka Seltzer is funny. You say 'Alka Seltzer' you get a laugh . . . Words with 'k' in them are funny", and he goes on to mention cup cakes, cookies, cucumbers and car keys as examples of the humorous potential of the K sound. "Cockroach is funny," he says, "not if you get 'em, only if you say 'em."

Finally, to move on from single-letter funniness to single-word humorous remarks, here are my two favourite one-word jokes.

The first comes in the play *Professional Foul* written for BBC television in 1977 by Tom Stoppard and featuring Peter Barkworth in the role of a football-loving philosopher who is giving a lecture at a linguistics conference in Prague. The philosopher stumbles on his way to the lectern, drops his lecture notes and hastily gathers them together again, but not in the right order. Still a little flustered, he begins his lecture: "Secondly . . ."

My other one-word joke came during a lunch with friends some time ago. Telling of the problems they were facing in a planned move from the English countryside to the centre of Madrid, they explained their worries about their large dog, which loved romping through the fields but would not like being cooped up in a city flat. They were horrified by my cynophobic suggestion that they have the dog put down, then get a smaller one for the flat, so I suggested they fly to Spain via Switzerland where they could have a painless assisted canicide performed. One of those present saw the joke: "Dognitas," he commented.

I suspect that none of the theories of humour can be stretched to cover either the humour of K-words or the dignity of Dognitas.

4
LAUGHTER AND HUMOUR

"Men have been wise in very different modes; but they have always laughed the same way."
Samuel Johnson, *Life of Cowley*, 1780

"Knock, knock."
"Who's there?"
"Little old lady."
"Little old lady who?"
"Oh, I didn't know you could yodel."

Like most knock-knock jokes, this type of humour is more likely to be greeted by wincing than by laughter, but as we have seen, laughter and humour have long been confused, though it can hardly be denied that they have a great deal in common. It was the uncontrolled outburst of laughter that aroused such indignation in Plato and others, yet we all feel an inner satisfaction at the appreciation of humour. Koestler's characteristically thoughtful explanation of the difference is simple: laughter is a physical reflex response while humour is an intellectual response. "Laughter", Koestler wrote, "prevents the satisfaction of biological drives, it makes a man equally incapable of killing or copulating; it deflates anger, apprehension, and pride." So let us see what we have really been able to discover about laughter.

Laughter seems to have evolved around seven million years ago, which was about the time that the first hominids and chimpanzees diverged from each other on their evolutionary timelines. Laughter is thus thought to have developed before speech and was one of the earliest forms of communication among early humans.

Whichever theory of humour one chooses to believe, we cannot know whether or by what period of time laughter preceded the evolution of humour, but even today laughter has a strong social aspect. It indicates a state of positive emotion not only in the person who laughs but also in whoever hears it (unless they are the one being laughed at) and laughing at the same time as others produces a shared feeling of goodwill.

Indeed, various studies have confirmed that we are far more likely to laugh when in the company of others than when we are alone. The American psychologist Robert Provine (1943–2019) wrote in *American Scientist* in 1996:

> Laughter is a decidedly social signal, not an egocentric expression of emotion. In the absence of stimulating media (television, radio or books), people are about 30 times more likely to laugh when they are in a social situation than when they are alone. Indeed people are more likely to smile or talk to themselves than they are to laugh when they are alone. Aside from the obvious implication that sociality can enhance laughter and perhaps one's mood, these observations indicate that laughter has a social function.

Provine and his students undertook a long study, surreptitiously listening to people in public places and noting instances of them laughing. They were surprised by their findings: "Contrary to our expectations we found that most conversational laughter is not a response to structured attempts at humour, such as jokes or stories. Less than 20 percent of the laughter in our sample was a response to anything resembling a formal effort at humour." More often than not, laughter was in response to a banal expression such as "Are you sure?" or "It was nice meeting you too."

Genuine humour is only one possible cause of laughter, and a relatively small one at that. We may laugh because we are embarrassed; we may laugh to show that we are in a good mood; we may laugh simply because other people are laughing (experiments with TV laughter tracks show how well this works); we may laugh because we are being tickled, which cannot be a purely physiological response or we would be able to tickle ourselves; we may laugh because we are nervous or stressed; we may laugh at others as a sign of contempt or superiority. What all these different types of laughter have in common and the question of whether they generate significantly different, identifiable laughing sounds are questions that have only recently begun to be addressed.

Before considering modern ideas, however, let's look at a fascinating contribution that dates back to 1898 and seems to have been almost forgotten. Entitled "On The Philosophy of Laughing", and written by the American writer, editor and philosopher Paul Carus for the philosophy journal *The Monist*, it is packed with good sense, original ideas and a not wholly successful attempt to explain why we laugh in the manner we do. One of this essay's best features is to get away at last from the critical attitude toward laughter that Plato had started and replace it with a much more positive message:

> Life is serious, and if we could see all the misery of life at once it would so oppress us that we would long to die. But because life is serious, and because we need a buoyant spirit to fight the struggle of life bravely, we need as a temporary relief from time to time a hearty laugh. The man who always laughs lacks seriousness, he is silly. Constant laughing betrays a fool. But a man who cannot laugh had better consult his physician. He is sick. He is devoid of that elasticity of spirit which is

so necessary for carrying the burden of life with ease and in good grace. He will not live long and had better attend to his last will.

More than a century after Carus had written those thoughtful comments in praise of laughter, John Morreall added a similar remark in his 1999 book *Comedy, Tragedy, and Religion*: "Human life is so full of failure, disappointment and suffering that without humour it would be unbearable."

Later in his essay, Paul Carus asks about the significance of the "reiterated shouting" which we experience in laughter, describing this as "a shout of triumph" or an expression of joy at a success, or at outwitting an adversary:

> "Ha!" we exclaim . . . If this Ha! be repeated several times, it forms a volley of ejaculations by which the whole breast begins to shake; and such a phenomenon is a regular laughter, which is nothing but the abbreviation of a triumphal shout. Translated into common parlance it means: "Hurrah, I have got the best of you and you are worsted." We laugh only at petty triumph. We never laugh when gaining a great victory, as on a battle-field; in such a case we set up a regular shout of triumph.

His attempt to differentiate different types of laughter from their sounds is less convincing:

> We may distinguish different kinds of laughter according to the sound. The laughter in *e*, "Hee-hee!", is the hiss and sneer of a trickishly gained victory; the laughter in *ey*, "Hey-hey!", expresses contempt at a worsted wretch who is now at our mercy; the laugh in *oh*, " Hohoh!" is a scoff of self-exaltation, as if to say, Is it possible that you could be so stupid; in *oo* it marks disgust. The object of our laughter is pooh-poohed by a "Hoo, hoo, hoo!"

which sounds like a protest that we won't have anything to do with the matter in question. The clearest and purest vowel, which is *ah*, is characteristic of the gallant victor, who does not intend to sneer or to scoff at his adversary, but simply enjoys a pure-hearted triumph. All kinds of laughter, however, equally participate in the initial consonant *h*; which denotes spirited pride and mirth, symbolizing the exulting breath of a swelling bosom and being in reality the attestation of a self-possessed mind, a victor and conqueror.

Sadly, Carus died in 1919, so was unable to tell us the meaning of the "yuck-yuck" with which Disney's Goofy often preceded a "hoo, hoo, hoo" as Goofy was not created until 1932. Since Carus wrote of the different laughing sounds, however, a difference between ha-ha and he-he has gradually emerged between American and English usage. According to the *Collins English Dictionary*, both countries use ha-ha in writing to represent the sound made while laughing, but in speech, the British sometimes say ha-ha to show that they are not amused by what you have said, or do not believe it. In Chinese, incidentally, ha-ha is generally a louder laugh than he-he, but he-he can also mean "you idiot".

There is currently an earnest debate on the difference between "haha" and "hehe" in Internet messages, but this seems very much in a state of flux so I shall not comment. The Chinese actress He Lan Dou, incidentally, is known as Haha He. Going back to the Samuel Johnson quotation with which we started this chapter, we must question whether he was right about people always having laughed the same way. Our attitude to laughter has certainly altered, but the meaning of a laugh and the way we do it may also have undergone a change over the years. Forget everything you may have read about Eskimo words for snow: those are clearly outdone by English words for laughing. The *Oxford English Dictionary* lists 46 verbs with "laugh" in their definition, of which "smile" (earliest citation 1300) and "laugh" itself (1175) are two of the oldest. Here are the others, with definitions, in chronological order of their earliest known use:

A Laughing Verbarium

hoat	1175	laugh
cackle	1225	chuckle, laugh, giggle
kench	1225	laugh loudly
buff	1297	explode or break into a laugh
bilauh	1357	laugh at; mock, deride
snort	1366	laugh loudly or roughly
twitter	1387	laugh in a somewhat suppressed way
fleer	1400	laugh in a coarse, impudent or unbecoming manner
chuck	1405	laugh
delude	1493	deride, mock, laugh at
giggle	1509	laugh continuously, in a manner not uproarious
keckle	1513	chuckle, laugh, giggle, checkle
deride	1530	laugh at in contempt or scorn
whinny	1530	laugh in a manner sounding like a horse
sneer	1553	laugh foolishly or smirkingly
crease	1588	become helpless with laughter
chuckle	1598	laugh in a suppressed manner
arride	1600	laugh or smile especially in mockery
outlaugh	1605	laugh down, deride, ridicule
nicker	1617	laugh loudly or shrilly

titter	1625	laugh in a somewhat suppressed or restrained way
checkle	1627	laugh violently or giddily
irride	1637	laugh at, to deride
whicker	1656	utter a half-suppressed laugh
goster	1673	laugh noisily
ridicule	1680	laugh at
roar	1689	laugh loudly and without restraint
snicker	1694	laugh in a half-suppressed or smothered manner
nicher	1700	laugh or snigger
snigger	1706	laugh in a half-suppressed manner
gawf	1719	laugh noisily
guffaw	1721	laugh noisily or boisterously
snirt	1724	laugh in a suppressed manner
grizzle	1746	grin or laugh, especially mockingly
snirtle	1786	laugh in a quiet, suppressed or restrained manner
smudge	1789	laugh quietly or to oneself
cacchinate	1824	laugh loudly or immoderately
snitter	1825	laugh in a suppressed, nervous manner
larf	1832	laugh
haw-haw	1833	laugh noisily or boisterously
yaw-haw	1836	laugh rudely or noisily
yock	1938	laugh loudly or uproariously
crack up	1942	burst out laughing
LOL	1997	laugh out loud

More than half these definitions contain a direct or implied criticism of laughter. Laughter as a form of mockery, laughing noisily, rudely or in an otherwise uncontrolled fashion are all disapproved of, which provides linguistic confirmation of Plato's doctrine of suspicion toward laughter in general.

All this, however, misses the point: Dr Johnson may have been right when he said that we have always laughed the same way, but the cause of that laughter has slowly but constantly been changing. Laughter may have begun seven million years ago as a contributor toward social bonding, but it developed a malicious side, which was what Plato and others objected to.

From Elizabethan comedy in the 16th century to Monty Python in the 20th, the art of making people laugh gradually became almost respectable – though as we shall see, there were continually changing limits beyond which humour was still seen as potentially disruptive.

Samuel Johnson himself was clearly not completely happy with laughter when he came to define that word in his *Dictionary of the English Language* (1755): "LAUGHTER, n.s. [noun, substantive]: Convulsive merriment; an inarticulate expression of sudden merriment." And he goes on to quote Edgar's speech from the start of Act 4 in Shakespeare's *King Lear*:

To be worst,
The lowest and most dejected thing of fortune,
Stands still in esperance; lives not in fear.
The lamentable change is from the best;
The worst returns to laughter.

He then rubs it in by adding a quotation from Sir Thomas Browne's *Pseudodoxia, or Vulgar Errors* (1672) which says disapprovingly: "The act of laughter, which is a sweet contraction of the muscles of the face, and a pleasant agitation of the vocal organs, is not merely voluntary, or totally within the jurisdiction of ourselves."

When considering these, we should, perhaps, always bear in mind Ambrose Bierce's definition of laughter in *The Devil's Dictionary* (1911): "Laughter, n. An interior convulsion, producing a distortion of the features and accompanied by inarticulate noises. It is infectious and, though intermittent, incurable."

A PSYCHOLOGIST WALKED INTO A BAR . . .

"Now this relaxation of the mind from work consists on playful words or deeds. Therefore it becomes a wise and virtuous man to have recourse to such things."

Thomas Aquinas (1225–1274)

The opening quotation from Aquinas's *Summa Theologica* often appears with the words "playful deeds and jokes", instead of "playful words or deeds". That is perhaps acceptable, as Aquinas spoke Italian and wrote in Latin, but it may give the impression that jokes were around in the 13th century though in fact the word "joke" was not recorded in the English language until 1670. So what was the first joke anyway? Before we think about that question, however, let's have a joke about Thomas Aquinas's *Summa Theologica*:

Thomas Aquinas walks into a bar, and the bartender asks how his work is going.

"I've been working on a treatise explaining Catholicism," Aquinas replies, "and I've even given it the perfect title: *Summa Theologica.* The trouble is, I've lost the manuscript and can't find it anywhere, which leaves me asking why God would inspire me to write it then let it be taken away."

"Ah well," the bartender says, "you win *summa*, you lose *summa*."

Since laughter probably predated speech, and writing only came very much later, we shall never know what was really the first joke, but several candidates have been put forward for the earliest example of a joke that was written down.

The oldest known joke was inscribed on a Sumerian cuneiform tablet that has been dated to around 1900 BC. Apparently, it was a comment on the rarity of a woman not farting in her husband's lap. Either it loses a great deal in the translation or it was not very funny.

Oddly enough, the Sumerians have also been credited with the earliest known "man walks into a bar" joke, only it wasn't a man but a dog: "A dog walked into a tavern and did not see anything, so said: 'Shall I open this one?'" Quite what the Sumerians made of this is a bit of a mystery, particularly on the question of what the dog was suggesting he might open. Some have pointed out that Sumerian taverns often housed brothels, so perhaps the dog was suggesting that he might see something if he opened a door to the lewd goings on. Another idea is that the dog's eyes were closed and he might see more if he opened them. It is generally agreed, however, that we know too little about Sumerian lifestyles and even less about Sumerian humour to make anything other than wild guesses.

Claims for the oldest joke that we do understand therefore date from the ancient Greek and Roman civilizations from which a few manuscripts have survived of early joke books. One of the earliest of these was written in Greek in third or fourth century Rome and was called *Philogelos* ("Love of Laughter"). Both classicists and comedians are on record as praising some of the 265 jokes in it as being similar to modern jokes or possible inspirations for recent comics, but the overwhelming impression gained by reading them all is of how unfunny they are.

As we mentioned in the first chapter of this book, the theme of eunuchs with hernias is common, as are jokes that make fun of intellectuals (or pedants, as some prefer to translate it). Here is one example:

> An intellectual, a bald man and a barber were travelling together and when they pitched camp, they agreed to take turns in staying awake to guard their possessions. The barber took the first watch and wanting to play a trick, he shaved the head of the sleeping intellectual whom he woke up when his watch was over. The intellectual rubbed his head on awakening and finding himself bare, said, "What a worthless barber: he has made a mistake and wakened the bald man instead of me."

I told you it wasn't funny, but we had clearly not made much progress by the time the earliest printed joke books began to appear more than a thousand years later. One such collection which became a Renaissance bestseller was an anthology called *Facetiae* by the Italian scholar Poggio Bracciolini (1380–1459). Much of his material was taken from ancient Greek or Roman sources, which means there is a good deal of overlap with *Philogelos*, but the style is more anecdotal, so the stories are longer and often even less funny. They are all given titles, such as "A Young Florentine Who Fornicated with His Step-Mother" or "A Jolly Story of a Woman Who Farted". As you may guess from these, crude themes are very common and farting stories particularly frequent.

While *Philogelos* had shown its scorn of absent-minded professors, *Facetiae* cast its net more widely, poking fun at stupidity throughout society. Take this one, for example, which has the title "A Man who carried his Plough on his Shoulder":

> Another uncouth peasant, Piero by name, had worked in his field until noon; his oxen were tired, and himself

spent with fatigue. About to make his way back to the village, he tied his plough upon the donkey, which he bestrode, after sending the oxen forward. Too heavily laden, the donkey faltered under the weight, and the rustic became at last aware that the poor beast could not hold out long. So he alighted, placed the plough on his own shoulder, and again mounted his donkey saying: "Thou canst get on now; for it is no longer thou, it is I who carry the plough."

This followed an equally long-winded story about a man who took several donkeys to market but whenever he counted them, he kept thinking he had lost one. This was because he always failed to count the donkey he was riding. Apparently such jokes had them rolling in the aisles in 15th-century Italy.

Feeble jokes, of course, have always been with us. The subject matter may change and evolve over time and we may not find eunuchs and hernias as funny as we once did, but that does not necessarily mean that the jokes have got better. The diversity of jokes of any age depends as much on fashion as the excellence of the joke itself and many types of joke undergo a period of popularity before they fade into obscurity until being rediscovered by a later generation. Any joke, to some extent at least, involves confounding expectations, whether they are expectations built up within the joke itself or expectations created by society or experience, so the effectiveness of a joke must depend also on the culture, the beliefs and the prejudices of the listener.

The evolution of jokes involving men walking into bars makes a revealing study. They all begin "A man (or guy) walks (or walked) into a bar" but how they continue may depend on the previous history of the joke itself. It has frequently been claimed that the very first such joke had appeared in an article by C. B. Palmer entitled "The Consummately Dry Martini" in the *New York Times* on 6 April 1952. That article in fact included two such jokes which it described as "some of the stories and formulas going around". Here is the first:

> A man walks into a bar and says he wants a *very, very* dry martini, 25 to 1. The bartender is a little startled but mixes it precisely. As he pours it out, he asks the customer: "Would you like a twist of lemon peel in it?"
>
> Customer pounds the bar and shouts: "Listen! When I want an asterisk obscenity lemonade, I'll ask for it."

The second one is equally unfunny:

> A man walks into a bar and says he wants a *very* dry martini, and he wants the man to mix it on top of the bar, so he can watch it. The bartender mixes it at about 7 to 1, chills it well and pours it out. The customer looks at it carefully and says: "Fine! That looks exactly right. Now I want you to mix me another just like it." The bartender does, and sets it out. This one the customer picks up and drinks and orders another.
>
> The bartender asks politely: "What about that one I mixed first? Aren't you going to drink that?"
>
> "Oh, no," says the man, "you can throw that away. I never can stand the taste of the first one."

Despite the low quality of these jokes, the man-walked-into-a-bar format caught on, with those opening words becoming a sort of shorthand for "I'm going to tell you a joke", which gets the listener in the right sort of mood to laugh. This may be useful if the joke is not very funny, such as this one: "A duck walks into a bar, orders a drink, and tells the bartender, 'Put it on my bill.'"

Another one that isn't very funny is also one of the shortest: "A man walked into a bar. Ouch!" This is just using the man-walked-into-a-bar format to mislead the listener about the nature of both "walking into" and "bar". This time it uses the conventional funny opening to turn into something that wasn't funny at all – at least for the man doing it.

So we have had the Sumerian dog, a man and a duck all walking into bars, but a Noah's ark of other animals have also been conscripted to add to the fun. Perhaps the one that was most responsible for enhancing the reputation of such bar jokes was the one with two horses. They order a couple of beers, sit down and start drinking when the barman comes over and asks if everything is all right. Are they comfortable? Are they enjoying the beer? Are they having a good time? After they respond positively to all questions, the barman asks, "Then why the long faces?"

The humour lies in its absurdity, but the horses joke is outdone by the polar bear who walked into a bar and asked for a gin and . . . , er, . . . a gin and . . . , er, a gin and . . . tonic. "Coming up, sir," says the bartender, "but why the long pause?" And the polar bear, of course, looks down at his paws and says, "I dunno. They've always been like that."

There are two points to make about the humour inherent in that one. First, it subtly and surprisingly improves on the horses joke by utilizing a physical feature of the animal to good punning effect, which makes it even more appreciated by anyone who already knows the equine version. The second point is something very unusual I have discovered when telling the joke: it provokes an even better reaction if the punchline is revealed at the start. Knowing that the joke will end with the words "I dunno. They've always been like that" makes it funnier when it actually does. Telling it in the conventional order is weaker because the listener gets the joke as soon as the bear looks at his paws, so the punchline comes too late.

Let's finish this section with two of my favourites and a recent addition. First, the longest of all bar-walking jokes: "An Englishman, an Irishman, a Welshman, a Scot, a Frenchman, a German, a Dane, a Russian, a Colombian, an American, a Dutchman, a Swede, an Australian . . ." You've probably got the idea by now – the list goes on with more than 200 items, then ends: " . . . tried to walk into an up-market bar but are denied entry because they don't have a Thai."

Reverting to classical times: "An ancient Roman walked in to a bar, held up two fingers and said, 'I'll have five beers please.'"

My last one, however, is funny because it has a typically comic start but the surprising finish is totally realistic: "A comedian, a politician and a hero walked into a bar and the barman said: 'Very pleased to see you, Mr Zelensky.'"

Having given this chapter the title of "A Psychologist Walked into a Bar", I searched for a joke beginning with those words but have been unable to find a good one. In 2007, a book by Thomas Cathcart and Daniel Klein was published with the intriguing title *Plato and a Platypus Walk into a Bar*. It was all about how jokes can illuminate philosophical ideas but the joke of the title was not revealed until the final words of the book: "Plato and a platypus walked into a bar. The bartender gave the philosopher a quizzical look, and Plato said, 'What can I say? She looked better in the cave.'"

When you think about it, that's hardly a walked-into-a-bar joke as it could have taken place anywhere, and anyway, it's about a philosopher not a psychologist. However, we have already talked about the philosophy of humour, so the idea of the current chapter was to move on to the contributions psychologists have made to our understanding of humour.

Until the late 19th century, psychology had not established itself as an independent science, awkwardly straddling the boundary between philosophy and medicine. The old philo-sophical confusion between humour and laughter then interfered with any attempt to develop a theory of humour that could be investigated by psychological experiments and it was not until around the 1970s that ideas were developed that made humour a valid area for research. Until then, anyone looking for a systematic treatment of aspects of humour struggled to find anything more authoritative than a curious work published in 1905 with the title *Der Witz und seine Beziehung zum Unbewußten* written by the founder of psychoanalysis himself, Sigmund Freud. It was not translated into English as "Jokes and Their Relation to the Unconscious" until 1960, when it confirmed to many that Freud did not have a great sense of humour.

The first section of Freud's book, which he calls "Analytic", is devoted to an extraordinarily cumbersome discussion on the techniques of jokes. This includes a large number of feeble jokes, mostly with a linguistic basis, all of which are followed by ponderous explanations of why they are funny. It all provides a glorious example of E. B. White's comparison between the dissection of humour with that of a frog. Freud's long section on double meanings provides an example of the gruesome innards and dead jokes as Freud reveals them.

Double meanings, he tells us, come in three varieties of which number three is explained as follows:

(c) Double meaning proper, or play upon words. This may be described as the ideal case of "multiple use". Here no violence is done to the word; it is not cut up into its separate syllables, it does not need to be subjected to any modification, it does not have to be transferred from the sphere it belongs to (the sphere of proper names, for instance) to another one. Exactly as it is and as it stands in the sentence, it is able, thanks to certain favourable circumstances, to express two different meanings.

He then gives several examples of this, including the following: "A doctor, as he came away from a lady's bedside, said to her husband with a shake of his head: 'I don't like her looks.' 'I've not liked her looks for a long time,' the husband hastened to agree."

It may have been funnier in German but in case we missed the joke, he explains: "The doctor was of course referring to the lady's condition; but he expressed his anxiety about the patient in words which the husband could interpret as a confirmation of his own marital aversion." *Danke*, Herr Doktor. *Sehr komisch.*

Yuck, yuck, yuck. And talking of marital aversion and yuck, yuck, here is a totally irrelevant Goofy joke: "Mickey and Minnie Mouse went to a marriage counsellor who, after an initial chat, said to Mickey, 'But just because Minnie is a bit stupid is no reason to want to divorce her.' 'I didn't say she was a bit stupid,' said Mickey. 'I said she was fucking Goofy.'"

The humour here, as Freud would have been the first to point out if he had heard the joke and analysed it, lies in the double meanings of "fucking" and "Goofy", the first being either a crude linguistic intensifier or the present participle of a verb meaning "to have sexual intercourse with", while Goofy can be either an animated colleague of the protagonists or an adjective indicating diminished intelligence. As we said earlier, yuck, yuck, yuck.

Meanwhile, back on Freud, the second section of his book, "Synthetic", discusses the motives of jokes and their role in the social process, and the final section, "Theoretical", purports to show the relationship jokes have with dreams and the subconscious, which had formed a large part of his earlier writings. So what Freud was trying to do was to fit jokes and joking into the framework he had built up to explain human motivation. Jokes, he said, are a way of letting out the feelings and thoughts that our conscious mind usually suppresses.

Such a theory, however, is applicable at best to a small proportion of jokes and even Freud himself admitted that it did not include ridiculous ones, which I think would include the Mickey–Minnie–Goofy example. So what exactly is a joke anyway?

The first definition of "joke" given by the *Oxford English Dictionary* is: "Something said or done to excite laughter or amusement", but we know that laughter is a complex phenomenon and not much of it is caused by jokes. So what about "amusement"?

Well, here the relevant definition in the *OED* is "Humour excited by something comical or funny". Pursuing this line of investigation, we discover that "comical" in this sense means "intentionally humorous or funny" and "funny" is "Humorous, comical, fun; causing laughter or amusement." We seem to be going round in circles here.

Since around 1970, psychologists have been trying to get to grips with jokes to find out what people find funny and why some jokes are funnier than others. A common experimental paradigm in that respect is to modify a joke by changing its introduction or punchline to make it more difficult to understand or less funny. The different versions of the joke are then presented to subjects who are asked to rate them on a humour scale.

One piece of research that used this paradigm was reported in a paper by R. S. Wyer and J. E Collins in 1992 ("A Theory of Humor Elicitation", *Psychological Review*, 99(4), 1992), which used the following joke:

> A young Catholic priest is walking through town when he is accosted by a prostitute. "How about a quickie for twenty dollars?" she asks. The priest, puzzled, shakes her off and continues on his way, only to be stopped by another prostitute. "Twenty dollars for a quickie," she offers. Again, he breaks free and goes on up the street. Later, as he is nearing his home in the country, he meets a nun. "Pardon me, sister," he asks, "but what's a quickie?" "Twenty dollars," she says. "The same as it is in town."

That joke was used to test a theory of humour maintaining that a joke had to involve two criteria to be funny: reinterpretation and diminishment. The first refers to the punchline implying a reinterpretation of something in the joke's introduction; the second refers to a diminishment in intelligence or status of a character in the joke. In the case of the nun, the diminishment consists in her being revealed as not as holy as one might have assumed, while the reinterpretation occurs in the meaning of "what's a quickie?" from "what is a quickie?" to "how much does a quickie cost?".

To test the effect of these aspects on perceived humour, the following changes were made in different versions of the joke:

1: The original joke.
2: The nun's response to "What's a quickie?" is changed to: "I'll show you, but it'll cost twenty dollars, just like in town."
3 and **4**: The nun is removed from the joke and replaced by another prostitute in both the original joke and the above version.
5: The joke now takes place at Hallowe'en, with the priest finally addressing a prostitute dressed as a nun.
6: The same as **5**, except that the prostitute's costume is explained before we arrive at the punchline.

When the "What's a quickie?" line is changed, the reinterpretation is eliminated or at least considerably reduced; when the "nun" turns out to be not a nun at all, the same happens to the diminishment aspect.

As one might expect, the changes were found to result in lower scores on perceived humour, but a related result reported in the same paper confirmed a more interesting hypothesis concerning the comprehension process involved in appreciating the joke. As the authors said: "less humor will be elicited if the concepts and knowledge required to reinterpret a stimulus event are either very easy or very difficult to identify than if they are moderately difficult to identify." In other words, making a joke difficult to comprehend increases its humour up to a point, but after that point, more complexity diminishes the humour. Again this was verified by making changes to jokes that made them easier, more difficult, or even impossible to understand.

Finally, Wyer and Collins also discuss the puzzling effects of hearing a joke one has heard before. As we all know, this is unlikely to make us laugh again, or at least to laugh as much as we did the first time, but we can still appreciate the humour. As many writers have pointed out, laughter is an emotional physiological reflex prompted by our intellectual perception of humour. When we hear a joke for a second or third time, our intellectual appreciation of the humour will not be diminished, but the reflex laughter is no longer produced.

In a recent conversation, I discovered a further elaboration of this phenomenon. After telling a rather poor joke to a friend, she said that it wasn't nearly as funny as the story about a rabbi and the Pope that I once told her. "I can't remember the joke, but I know it was very funny," she said. I couldn't remember it either, but we both laughed. I am still unsure whether this was social laughter, or laughter at the fact that we found a joke we couldn't remember funny, or laughter at the memory of previous laughter. More research is clearly necessary, but the psychology of jokes is still clearly in its infancy. As we wait for it to grow, however, the neurology of humour has been making significant strides, as we shall discover in the next chapter.

ALL IN THE MIND

"I like nonsense: it wakes up the brain cells."

Dr Seuss

A young man was having problems deciding on his future career. Should he be a neurologist or a novelist? He asked a friend for advice and the friend told him to toss a coin, saying: "Basically, it's heads or tales."

Until recently, we have not had much idea what goes on in the brain when we laugh at something. Indeed, we have, until recently, not had much idea of what happens in the brain at all. The task of explaining humour therefore fell mainly to philosophers and psychologists but, as we have seen, they came up with, at best, partial theories and explanations. In recent years, however, that has begun to change as neurologists have increasingly developed techniques to examine the human brain in detail.

Until the late 20th century, most of what we knew about the brain came from observations of people who had suffered injuries to that organ. The functions of different brain regions was deduced from observing the deficiencies resulting from damage to such areas.

The old theory, generally held until around 1980, was linked to the idea that the two hemispheres of the brain were responsible for different activities: the left side was thought to be the domain of language and logic, while the right side was creative and artistic, which included responsibility for humour appreciation. For the most part, that idea is now rejected or at least considered far too simplistic, yet several studies on humour seemed to support it to some extent at least.

In one study of subjects who had suffered localized brain injury, damage to the left hemisphere was found to have little effect in appreciating humour, but damage to the right resulted in unpredictable changes. Another study confirmed that right-hemisphere damaged patients had a greater tendency to choose total non-sequiturs as the funniest captions to cartoons and were liable to be unable to explain the humour, even when presented with the correct caption.

A possible explanation of this confusion was offered in the idea that correct interpretation of a joke can be a two-stage procedure: first, the building up of expectations based on the natural interpretation of the set-up, then the re-assessment of everything when the punchline confounds those expectations. A non-sequitur ending can be perceived as a surprise and seen as just as humorous as the correct ending because the damaged right hemisphere cannot resolve the incongruity in either case.

This interpretation may be supported by a case reported in 1998 concerning a patient undergoing brain surgery for epileptic seizures. As was common in such cases, the patient was conscious during the procedure while electrical stimulation was applied to various areas of her brain to locate the precise place where surgery was necessary. When such stimulation was applied to one small area of the left frontal lobe, it consistently provoked genuine laughter. When asked why she was laughing, the patient was reported to have described whatever she was looking at as "funny", even thought there was no humour in it at all.

As with the earlier subjects with right-frontal-lobe damage, she was apparently finding something funny without being able to explain why. Interviewed about her experience later, however, she said her response had nothing to do with what she was looking at but her genuine laughter was caused by her laughing at something that wasn't funny.

Hang on a moment – that explanation is really weird. If she is laughing because she thinks it is funny that she is laughing at nothing, what caused the laughter that she is laughing at in the first place? She saw something that wasn't funny and laughed at it, then laughed because she thought it funny that she was laughing. Once again these relationships between a patient's behaviour and activation of certain parts of the brain emphasize the difference between humour and laughter: under normal circumstances, the first is an intellectual response to a type of incongruity, while the second is the emotional, physiological response to the intellectual realization. In the above case, however, it seems that the physiological response of laughter came before the intellect worked out a reason for it.

The trouble with all those experiments is that the sample is highly selective, being restricted either to brain-damaged individuals or people undergoing surgery and is therefore atypical of the general population. At the start of the 21st century, however, all that began to change as the science of brain scanning for the first time allowed perfectly normal people to look at cartoons, listen to jokes and even watch funny television programmes or films and make comments on them while having their brains precisely scanned. The development of magnetic resonance imaging techniques in neuroscience then opened up many possibilities to investigate the brain more deeply.

Functional magnetic resonance imaging (fMRI) is a technique that measures brain activity by detecting changes associated with a type of blood flow. This technique is based on the fact that cerebral blood flow and neuronal activation in the brain are closely connected. When a certain brain part is working, the blood flow to that region also starts to increase. We can therefore measure brain activity by detecting changes in blood flow.

The discovery that brain activity correlates with blood flow was made in the 1890 but it took a century before an effective way of using that finding was developed. Quite how this is done need not bother us, but for anyone interested, the basic component of an fMRI scanner is a very powerful electromagnet that can detect the magnetic signals from the hydrogen nuclei in water. Active brain areas need more oxygen, which is delivered by haemoglobin in red blood cells, so the greater the activity in any area, the greater the blood flow and the greater the magnetic signal from the hydrogen nuclei, which is what the fMRI measures and displays in images showing different intensities in various colours.

The first use of fMRI in humour research was a great success, pinpointing the precise areas of the brain that were activated by certain jokes. It was written up in an unpretentious two-page paper by Vinod Goel and Raymond J. Dolan in *Nature Neuroscience* in 2001 with the title "The functional anatomy of humor: segregating cognitive and affective components". Explaining their experimental method, the researchers say: "We scanned 14 right-handed normal subjects using event-related fMRI while they listened to jokes." The term "event-related" simply meant that a subject's cognitive processes had been separated into discrete points in time (referred to as "events"), which allowed differentiation of their associated fMRI signals. In this case, the events consisted of 60 jokes divided equally between "phonological jokes" (based on puns or double meanings) and "semantic jokes" based on understanding and knowledge of the world. The examples they gave in the paper were as follows:

Phonological: Q. Why does the golfer wear two pairs of pants? A. Because he got a hole in one.
Semantic: Q. What do engineers use for birth control?
A. Their personalities.

For comparison purposes, the subjects were also told the jokes with changed punchlines that were not funny: for example, "It was a very cold day" for the golfing joke and "The pill" for the birth-control joke. The brain scans were then examined to see what differences they showed between semantic and phonological jokes or between funny and unfunny ones.

Subjects were also asked to say whether they found each joke funny and to rate it for funniness on a scale of 1 to 5. The results were intriguing and very much confirmed both earlier thoughts about humour and the earliest results of brain scans.

Phonological jokes based on puns or double meanings were shown to result in greater activity in subjects' left inferior prefrontal cortex, which earlier studies had shown were involved in phonological (sound-related) processing. Semantic jokes, however, produced increased activity in bilateral posterior temporal lobes, which had previously been shown to be active in language processing. Many jokes, of course, contain both phonological and semantic aspects, but this study was restricted to jokes that were purely one type or the other. For example: "Q: What's orange and sounds like a parrot? A: A carrot" is purely phonological but "Why did Cleopatra bathe in milk? Because she couldn't find a cow tall enough for a shower!" is semantic, with nothing phonological about it at all. The parrot/carrot joke would thus have been appreciated by the left inferior prefrontal cortex of anyone hearing it, while the Cleopatra/cow story would have headed for the bilateral posterior temporal lobes.

The funniest jokes of either type were reported to activate the medial ventral prefrontal cortex, which had previously been seen to be active in people when they are receiving rewards. This last finding, which was confirmed in several later studies, suggested that humour perception, which often takes the form of laughter, is a rewarding experience – something that all of us, with the possible exception of Plato and his humour-sceptic followers, have suspected for thousands of years.

Amusingly, Goel reported that in this study, they deliberately chose only mildly funny jokes, because they did not want their subjects bursting out laughing, which could result in head movements that might interfere with accurate fMRI readings. In general, their results were supported and expanded by later research of a similar nature, including a study in which subjects looked at cartoons and another study involving participants watching episodes of *Seinfeld* or *The Simpsons*. In the latter study by William Kelley and Joseph Moran in 2004, the posterior temporal lobes (which had previously been seen to be active in the perception of incongruities) were seen to light up when the subject got the point of the joke, while the amygdala (which has a strong role in controlling emotions) was seen to be active during laughter.

The picture grew still more complex with a study by Watson, Matthews and Allman in 2006 in which subjects looked at *Far Side* cartoons by Gary Larson while undergoing fMRI scans. Some of the cartoons had captions while others were purely visual and the scans perhaps unsurprisingly showed clear differences between brain activity between the two types: high-level visual areas were activated during visual humour whereas classic language areas were activated in response to language-dependent cartoons with captions. The results also showed that both types activated a common area that included the amygdala and midbrain regions, reflecting the euphoric component of humour.

To throw two more brain areas into the humorous mix, however, they also identified activity in the anterior cingulate cortex and fronto-insular cortex, which are known to have evolved more recently. The paper's authors conclude: "These results suggest that humor may have coevolved with another cognitive specialization of the great apes and humans: the ability to navigate through a shifting and complex social space."

As if the involvement of all these different brain regions in humour perception was not complicated enough, a piece of research in 2016 added yet another wrinkle when it occurred to two researchers at the University of Southern California to investigate the difference between humour perception and humour generation. For that purpose, Ori Amir and Irving Biederman, who had already used fMRI scans in previous studies of humour, recruited a number of successful professional comedians, promising amateur stand-up comics and a group of non-comedians, and asked them to write captions to cartoon pictures which had had their original captions and all other verbal material removed. Before each cartoon was presented to them, the subjects were given one of three instructions: to generate a humorous caption; to generate a bland, non-humorous caption; or just to look at the picture without adding any caption. The subjects were also asked to rate the humour of each caption generated under the first condition and ratings were also obtained from an independent group. The fMRI scans were investigated for differences between brain activity in the three conditions, differences between highly rated captions and low-rated, and differences between the professional, the amateur and the non-comedian groups.

The most intriguing finding was between the professionals and non-professionals. For all groups, the results identified activity in the medial prefrontal cortex and the temporal association regions of the brain when jokes were produced, but the results showed that the more experienced someone was at doing comedy, the more activation there was in the temporal lobe. This is known to be the region of the brain that mainly functions around hearing and selective listening and is thus vitally important for understanding speech and visual information. It is also the area where abstract information, semantic information and creative associations are all put together in a meaningful way. It mainly receives sensory information such as signals and speech from the ears to form the basis for our understanding or comprehension. In fact, if we did not have a temporal lobe in our brain, we would not even be able to understand that someone was talking to us. This lobe is special because it interprets all the different types of sounds transmitted from the sensory receptors of the ears.

By contrast, the prefrontal cortex, which the unprofessional groups were relying on, is responsible for planning complex behaviour and decision-making. Funniness ratings were also found to be higher when temporal regions of the brain were used.

Ori Amir summed it up by saying that: "The more experience you have doing comedy, the less you need to engage in the top-down control and the more you rely on your spontaneous associations." Like so many other mental activities, you learn to do it almost without thinking instead of having to work it out every time. This finally begins to explain why spontaneous humour tends to be funnier than humour that has been laboriously worked out: it comes with experience when our humour production is able to move on to a more creatively efficient part of the brain.

For centuries, philosophers, moralists and psychologists had tried to get to grips with the nature of humour but reached few conclusions. Only when neurologists entered the fray with fMRI scans was progress made, but many questions remain to be answered. The results outlined above identify the parts of the brain we use in performing the activities we must undertake in order to find something funny, such as recognizing an incongruity or switching from one interpretation of something to another. We have also made great strides in discovering which region of the brain is responsible for causing the physiological reaction of laughter and we have confirmed that jokes makes us feel good. Yet we still cannot point to a specific location in the brain where humour resides.

Perhaps "humour" is just a convenient umbrella term to cover a multitude of sensations that have a feel-good effect. The search for the nature of humour may be an illusion, which would, of course, explain why so many diverse theories of humour have been proposed. It could be that all of them are right, setting off different parts of the brain but all ending by provoking laughter.

"The brain is a wonderful organ; it starts working the moment you get up in the morning and does not stop until you get into the office."

Robert Frost

EVOLUTION

*"The pathways that have led to our evolution are quirky,
improbable, unrepeatable and utterly unpredictable."*
                                    Stephen Jay Gould, *I Have Landed*

Before leaving the theory of humour, we should return to the
matter of its evolution, so here's an evolutionary joke:

One day, a zookeeper was astonished to see that a
chimpanzee was not only reading a book but seemed to
be reading two books at once: the Bible and Darwin's
Origin of Species. The ape, however, explained all: "I'm
trying to figure out if I'm my brother's keeper, or my
keeper's brother."

Every human society throughout history, and probably also
apes, has shown a capacity for laughing, so we need to ask what
evolutionary advantages it confers on us and what role humour
has played in the development of mankind. And as we shall see,
primates are not the only creatures that display the traits we
associate with humour.

In the second half of the 19th century, when science was
still coming to terms with Darwinian evolution, one of the
competing ideas was that of replication theory. The idea behind
this was that the process an embryo goes through as it proceeds
to adulthood replicates that of its species as it slowly transformed
over a great time period. The German zoologist Ernst Haeckel
(1834–1919) was a major proponent of this idea, which he

expressed succinctly in a phrase that became strongly associated with him: "Ontogeny recapitulates phylogeny", meaning that the development of an individual mimics the development of the species as a whole.

Even Darwin himself thought this a little far-fetched and saw little evidence for it, and as theories of evolution and genetics were developed, Haeckel's theory was considered at best irrelevant and at worst completely misguided. Humour, however, is one area in which there are some grounds for thinking that ontogeny may indeed recapitulate phylogeny. The following comparison table may help you judge how much you agree with that.

ONTOGENY	PHILOGENY
At around the age of three months, a child's first smile develops.	All great apes display an expression similar to smiling, which suggests the smile evolved even before we became human and came well before language.
From a very early age, babies like being tickled.	Darwin pointed out that the most ticklish parts of the body are the areas most prone to attack by predators. Tickling may thus have evolved as training for predator avoidance.
At the age of seven or eight months, there is evidence that children use their faces and voices to provoke laughter in adults.	Humour is widely held to help social bonding and thus is thought to have played a role in the development of society.
Toddlers show the ability to spot incongruity very early in life and to find it funny.	The detection of incongruity is of importance in the development of understanding in general and science in particular.
Children show the first signs of toilet humour at the same time as toilet training.	Jokes in Ancient Rome have been seen to contain a high proportion of jokes about eunuchs and hernias.
Visual humour is apparent in children long before their language skills have developed enough to appreciate more sophisticated language-based jokes.	Visual slapstick humour was very common in the theatre and early films before our tastes grew more sophisticated.

For a long time, in our typically anthropocentric arrogance, humans thought they were the only creatures with a sense of humour. In a sophisticated sense, that may be true, but we are certainly not the only animals to laugh and smile. The idea that laughter is a characteristic only of humans goes back to Aristotle and that view was unquestioned for two millennia.

In 1938, the Dutch cultural historian Johan Huizinga wrote, in his thoughtful work *Homo Ludens*, on the role of play in our development: "It is worth noting that the purely physiological act of laughing is exclusive to man, whilst the significant function of play is common to both men and animals. The Aristotelian *animal ridens* characterizes man as distinct from the animal almost more absolutely than homo sapiens." In other words, it is not so much our wisdom as our laughter that makes us different from other animals.

Even Darwin, however, in 1872 in his book *The Expression of the Emotions in Man and Animals* had drawn attention to the similarity in facial expressions and the sounds made by humans and monkeys when they are joyous. "The interrupted, laughing or tittering sounds made by man and by various kinds of monkeys when pleased, are as different as possible from the prolonged screams of these animals when distressed," he wrote, and though cautious about describing monkeys as laughing, he had no doubts that they smiled. More recently, however, researchers have detected something closely akin to laughter in a very different animal: the rat.

For some time, it has been known that rats like being tickled, but in 2016 researchers in Berlin made two breakthroughs in furthering our knowledge: the first was to establish a neurological basis for the rats' joy and the second was the discovery that the tickling provoked laughter. The reason the second of these had not been discovered before was that a rat's laughter consists of an ultrasonic chirping that had to be detected on sophisticated equipment before anyone became aware of it.

To investigate all this, Michael Brecht and Shimpei Ishiyama at the Humboldt University of Berlin inserted electrodes into the part of the rat brain that responds to touch on the skin. When the rats were tickled on their bellies, certain neurons fired intensely, though back-tickling and tail-tickling produced much weaker responses. When the same neurons in the brain were stimulated with the electrodes, the rats chirped in the same way even though they were not being tickled. Perhaps the most surprising result of all was that if the rats were subjected to something that caused anxiety before they were tickled, they did not laugh.

As Darwin had pointed out in the case of a child being tickled: "the mind must be in a pleasurable condition; a young child, if tickled by a strange man, would scream from fear." We now know that something very similar is true of rats.

In the timetable of evolution, rats and humans diverged about 75 million years ago, while the last common ancestor of humans and chimpanzees existed around 7 million years ago. It seems that laughter has been around for even longer than we thought.

What all this theorizing makes clear is that there are still many things we do not understand about humour. Are we right in assuming that jokes, slapstick and tickling have something in common other than the fact that they can all make us laugh? Where does social laughter, when nothing funny has happened at all, fit into this humour spectrum? What can we say about jokes or situations that do not make us laugh though we insist that we find them funny? And is smiling just a mild case of laughter?

Since 1862, however, even the last of those questions has developed a further wrinkle – a wrinkle around the eyes, in fact. In that year, the French anatomist Guillaume Duchenne de Boulogne identified the difference between various types of smile. Duchenne was one of the world's first neurologists and spent much of his time pursuing a misguided idea that facial expressions could reveal key information about a person's soul. His research in pursuit of that theory consisted of delivering electric shocks to patients by the means of electrodes inserted beneath the skin of their faces and seeing what expressions would result. While doing this, however, he made the important discovery that there are two main types of smile.

A genuine smile, or Duchenne smile as it is known after its discoverer, is a natural smile that spreads over the whole face including wrinkles round the eyes; a non-Duchenne smile is the sort of fake smile one puts on when asked to say "cheese" by a photographer, or when one pretends to like someone. In a non-Duchenne smile, the lips curl upwards, but these are no wrinkles around the eyes. For many years, it was thought that the orbicularis oculi muscles, which cause the cheeks to rise and the eyes to wrinkle, were not under a person's voluntary control so a Duchenne smile could not be faked, but in 2009 research showed that some people can indeed fake natural smiles. Not only was such a thing possible but when people successfully faked a Duchenne smile, it made them happy.

A later study also showed that advertisements featuring a model with a Duchenne smile were more likely to persuade people to have a high opinion of the product and buy it than the same adverts with a non-Duchenne smiling model.

To further confuse the picture, it has also been shown, perhaps unsurprisingly, that people can also fake non-Duchenne smiles, which I think means that you can successfully pretend to be pretending to be amused when your amusement is in fact genuine.

Even though he has genuine smiles named after him, Guillaume Duchenne was not the first to differentiate between types of smile. James Beattie, the 18th-century Scottish philosopher whom we met as being the first to suggest that incongruity is an essential part of humour, expressed a related thought in his 1779 essay on laughter:

> Of the innocent and agreeable smile there are two
> sorts. The one proceeds from the risible emotion, and
> has a tendency to break out into laughter. The other
> is the effect of good humour, complacency and tender

affection. This last sort of smile renders a countenance amiable in the highest degree.

As for types of laughter, Beattie had even stronger views:

> There are different kinds of Laughter. As a boy, passing by night through a church-yard, sings or whistles to conceal his fear even from himself; so there are men, who, by forcing a smile, endeavour sometimes to hide from others, and from themselves too perhaps, their malevolence or envy. Such laughter is unnatural. The sound of it offends the ear; the features distorted by it offend the eye. A mixture of hypocrisy, malice, and cruel joy thus displayed on the countenance, is one of the most hateful sights in nature, and transforms the "human face divine" into the visage of a fiend, Similar to this is the smile of a wicked person pleasing himself with the hope of accomplishing his evil purposes . . . Laughter that makes man a fiend or monster, I have no inclination to analyse. My inquiries are confined to that species of it, which is at once natural and innocent.

Guillaume Duchenne, I feel, could not have put it better himself, despite his habit of conducting experiments on the severed heads of guillotine victims to see what contorted facial expressions he could induce with shocks from electrodes.

Attitudes to smiling, laughter and humour in general may have altered over time, and have also evolved differently in different places. As much of humour is based on language, it is hardly surprising that many jokes cannot be translated from one language into another, which has therefore resulted in national differences in their characteristic types of humour. Even when countries share the same language, however, their cultures may differ considerably, affecting the type of humour they enjoy or even understand. George Bernard Shaw is generally credited as having described Britain and America as "two countries divided by a common language" (though that precise quotation is not to be found in his published writings), but that quip is perhaps nowhere more credible than in their respective realms of humour.

Everyone seems to agree that there are differences between American and British humour (quite apart from the way in which they spell the word "humo(u)r"), but no two accounts agree on what these differences are or where they came from. Perhaps the most convincing answer came from Stephen Fry in a session at the book festival in Hay-on-Wye in 2009: "All great British comic heroes are failures," he said in response to a question from the audience. "We [the British] glory in our failure. We celebrate it." He characterized British comic heroes as predominantly lower middle-class, who are embarrassed by their own lack of dignity. By contrast, the main characters in US comedies are ordinary types who are great at wisecracking. As Fry put it, they are "not characters at all, just brilliant repositories of fantastic killer one-liners". Americans are brought up in the belief that they may one day become President, while their British counterparts are indoctrinated to believe that it is unlikely they will amount to anything much. As a result, Americans tend to celebrate success while Britons love a failure and those are predominantly the attitudes reflected in their comedies.

Some good examples of this have been seen when a British comedy was re-made for the American market. A typical example was *Fawlty Towers*, which many would say is the funniest comedy ever seen on British television. At least three attempts were made to create versions for the US market, but all that can be said is that they ranged from disappointing to disastrous: *Snaveley* (1978) got as far as a pilot TV movie but failed to result in a series; *Amanda's* (1983) was cancelled after ten episodes were shown of a planned thirteen; *Payne* (1999) did still worse with only eight programmes transmitted. The main problem all of them ran up against was in creating a version of John Cleese's character of Basil Fawlty, who brilliantly suited the British archetype, never losing his swaggering confidence although all his ideas fell apart. One could hardly imagine anything less like the lovable, witty guy-next-door role demanded in a US sitcom.

After that experience, *The Office* (UK) was transformed into *The Office* (US) with more foresight and the embarrassingly appalling and incompetent character of David Brent (played by Ricky Gervais) was turned into Steve Carell's far more benign, though equally incompetent, Michael Scott. He made just as many mistakes as David Brent, but was nowhere near as rude to his employees and the viewer tended to feel sympathy for him rather than laughing at his predicament when disaster struck.

Ricky Gervais himself wrote about the differences between American and British humour in an article in *Time* magazine in 2011 in which he explained the necessary changes in *The Office* when it crossed the Atlantic:

> We had to make Michael Scott a slightly nicer guy, with a rosier outlook to life. He could still be childish, and insecure, and even a bore, but he couldn't be too mean. The irony is of course that I think David Brent's dark descension and eventual redemption made him all the more compelling. But I think that's a lot more palatable in Britain . . . Brits almost expect doom and gloom so to start off that way but then have a happy ending is an unexpected joy.

To emphasize the point he was making, he added:

> Network America has to give people a reason to like you not just a reason to watch you. In Britain we stop watching things like *Big Brother* when the villain is evicted. We don't want to watch a bunch of idiots having a good time. We want them to be as miserable as us. America rewards up front, on-your-sleeve niceness. A perceived wicked streak is somewhat frowned upon.

So is the main difference between us caused by Americans being predominantly optimistic compared with the pessimism of the British? A very different point of view was expressed by the British writer and politician Sir Harold Nicolson in his essay "The English Sense of Humour" of 1946, arguing that British humour resulted from the special qualities and defects that form the British character and temperament. He listed ten such qualities, starting with "good humour and tolerance", "an affection for nature", and "a fund of common sense", and ending with "self-consciousness", "laziness" and "optimism". He then went on to list what he saw as ten components of English humour and tried, with varying degrees of success, to ally the two lists. His arguments for "optimism" were among the least convincing.

"Human beings", he wrote,

> ... seek instinctively to defend themselves against the
> unhappiness cause by the contrast between the real
> and the ideal, between the finite and the infinite. The
> mystic and the idealist seek to protect themselves by
> concentrating upon the infinite; the realist seeks to give
> to the finite the validity of the infinite; but the "practical
> humourist", that is the man to whom a sense of humour
> has become part of his attitude toward life, adopts for
> his protection a mood of general good-humour, which
> enables him to take an indulgent view both of the finite
> and the infinite and to see absurdity everywhere.

The English sense of humour, Nicolson told us, operates as "a defence mechanism against the alarming, the unfamiliar, the horrible, the dread of ridicule, or the pain derived from intellectual and social superiority in others".

Or, I might suggest, we just find the sight of Basil Fawlty hitting the hapless Manuel, or David Brent seriously performing a ridiculous dance, very funny. They are both very much part of the evolution of absurdist humour that has particularly taken place in the 20th century. P. G. Wodehouse wrote his first Jeeves and Wooster novel in 1920 (of which much more later in our chapter on comic novels) and J. B. Morton took over the Beachcomber column in the *Daily Express* in 1924, which he continued writing for the next 50 years. Both of these introduced a style of surreal humour that had rarely if ever been seen before and, most remarkably, both apparently emerged fully formed out of nowhere. Their styles remained the same half a century after they began and still stood out as funnier than those of any other writer. My favourite J. B. Morton quotation, incidentally, is a line he is said to have added to a Beachcomber column in the 1930s when a sub-editor asked him if he could provide three or four more lines to fill the available space. "Yes," said Morton immediately, "take this down." And he offered the following: "Erratum. In my article on the Price of Milk, 'Horses' should have read 'Cows' throughout."

The inherent absurdity of Wodehouse and Morton inspired *The Goon Show* on the radio, which in turn inspired the humour of *Monty Python's Flying Circus* on television which John Cleese carried over to *Fawlty Towers*.

As we have seen, the theories advocated by the philosophy of humour have evolved a great deal over the centuries, but there is one more important aspect that can help put some of the arguments into context – or perhaps confuse them even further: the difference between wit and humour.

Nowadays, the usual distinction made between wit and humour is that wit consists of a subtle, clever comment stemming from an intellectual process, while humour is a spontaneous and natural guttural process. This has frequently been identified as the difference between the American and British sense of humour: Americans are more humorous, the British are wittier. The American liking for slapstick is based on humour, while the British liking for clever dialogue reflects their love of wit. Wit makes fun of others and laughs at them; humour laughs with them.

On that basis, while many may applaud the wittiest lines from Oscar Wilde to John Cleese and beyond, there have been times when wit was viewed with suspicion or even contempt. The English philosopher John Locke, in his *Essay Concerning Human Understanding* (1689), launched a surprisingly rational criticism of wit in a section on "The Difference of Wit and Judgment" (Chapter 11, Section 2):

> Being able nicely to distinguish one thing from another, where there is but the least difference, consists, in a great measure, the exactness of judgment, and clearness of reason, which is to be observed in one man above another. And hence perhaps may be given some reason of that common observation, – that men who have a great deal of wit, and prompt memories, have not always the clearest judgment or deepest reason. For WIT lying most in the assemblage of ideas, and putting those together with quickness and variety, wherein can be found any resemblance or congruity, thereby to make up pleasant pictures and agreeable visions in the fancy; JUDGMENT, on the contrary, lies quite on the other side, in separating carefully, one from another, ideas wherein can be found the least difference, thereby to avoid being misled by similitude, and by affinity to take one thing for another.

In other words, the speed and immediacy of wit is its greatest enemy as it interferes with the process of thinking things through slowly and rationally.

Thomas Hobbes expressed a similar thought in his *Elements of Law, Natural and Politic* (1640, Chapter 10, section 5):

> There is another defect of the mind, which men call *levity,* which betrayeth also mobility in the spirits, but in excess. An example whereof is in them that in the midst of any serious discourse have their minds diverted to every little jest or witty observation; which maketh

them depart from their discourse by a parenthesis, and from that parenthesis by another, till at length they either lose themselves, or make their narration like a dream, or some studied nonsense. The passion from whence this proceedeth is curiosity, but with too much equality and indifference; for when all things make equal impression and delight, they equally throng to be expressed.

The virtue opposite to this defect is *gravity,* or steadiness; in which the end being the great and master delight, directeth and keepeth in the way thereto all other thoughts.

The extremity of dullness is that natural folly which may be called *stolidity;* but the extreme of levity, though it be natural folly distinct from the other, and obvious to every man's observation, I know not how to call it.

When the American cartoonist Bill Watterson created the *Calvin and Hobbes* comic strip in 1985, he named the tiger character after Thomas Hobbes, partly on the grounds that the tiger took a similarly dim view of mankind as that of the philosopher. Thomas Hobbes, after all, is famed for saying that the condition of man is a "condition of war against everyone" and that life without government would be "solitary, poor, nasty, brutish and short".

Perhaps Thomas Hobbes's views on humour were coloured by his colourless, philosophical personality. Calvin and Hobbes, however, were very funny. So let's devote the rest of this book to examining some of the leading exponents of humour over the ages and look at where they have left us.

PART TWO

HUMOUR IN PRACTICE

8
COMEDIANS

"Everything is changing. People are taking their comedians seriously and the politicians as a joke."
                                            Will Rogers (November 1932)

Two cannibals are eating a comedian. One looks at the other and says: "Does this taste funny to you?"

Despite the undeniable fact that humour has been a part of us for thousands if not millions of years, the role of a professional comedian, whose job it is to make us laugh, was slow in coming and even slower to gain respectability. As we have already seen, the word "comedy" originally had no direct connection with humour but was applied to any stage play that was not a tragedy. From around 1580, any writer, especially a playwright, who composed such an entertainment was thus called a "comedian". In 1603, according to the *Oxford English Dictionary*, the word's use was widened to include any actor who appeared in a comedy but its first use in the modern sense of an entertainer who tells jokes was not seen until 1860. As for "stand-up comedian", the earliest citation for that phrase in the *OED* is from as late as 1966.

Yet in ancient Greece and Rome, such jokesters were known, though generally frowned upon by the ruling classes and classified alongside mimics and jugglers as being of low social standing. One word the Romans used of such people was *scurra*, meaning a professional buffoon or clown who was seen as a parasite in the pay of a wealthy person. The low esteem in which such comedians were held can be found in the same word's modern English derivative: "scurrilous".

Noble Greeks in ancient times liked to invite buffoons to entertain them at dinner, so the comedian fraternity was little better than scroungers who turned up uninvited and told jokes in exchange for a free meal. No transcripts of their performances have survived, of course, but such accounts as there are suggest that the jokes contained a great deal of mockery.

Placing comedians low in the class structure was something the Greeks and Romans had in common. Aristotle himself had advised, in his *Rhetoric*, that a gentleman should be careful in selecting what jests he employs: "Some are becoming to a gentleman, others are not; see that you choose such as become you. Irony better befits a gentleman than buffoonery; the ironical man jokes to amuse himself, the buffoon to amuse other people." In ancient Rome, Cicero advised keeping wit respectable and ensuring that humour was moralistic. He also stressed the importance of maintaining gravitas and prudence, even when joking.

As time went on, crude humour and personal attacks thus became less frequent and were increasingly seen as unacceptable. Roman law even forbade ridiculing citizens by name and the performance of comedy was mostly restricted to festivals with clowns and mimes generally consisting of foreigners, slaves or former slaves.

This classical attitude to humour set the standards for the Middle Ages, when the influence of the Christian Church started to play an increasingly important role. Laughter was seen as a violation of the rules of good behaviour and something to be repressed or stifled. At its most extreme, this attitude forms the theme of Umberto Eco's *The Name of the Rose*, as we discussed in Chapter 2, but a similar idea was expressed much earlier and more succinctly in *A Book of Burlesques* by the American humourist H. L. Mencken, first published in 1916 and showing that the mediaeval suspicion of humour had lasted through the centuries. In a chapter titled "The Jazz Webster", he provides alternative definitions to a number of words including the following: "CREATOR. A comedian whose audience is afraid to laugh." He goes on to list three proofs of God's humour: "democracy, hay fever, any fat woman". My favourite definition from this chapter, incidentally, is the one he gives for ADULTERY: "Democracy applied to love".

It has been suggested that three people are needed for a good joke: one telling the joke, one laughing at it, and one being laughed at (though the third may be the same person as one of the first two). It was the third of these people that caused the Church such concern, for laughing at someone was perceived as not a good thing to do. There was, however, a spectrum of views on the matter of laughter in general. The extremists at one end thoroughly disapproved of it; the extremists at the other end considered laughter a sign of joy, which therefore made it always virtuous at least to some extent, while the middle ground was taken by those seeking a compromise, approving of smiling, controlled laughter and decent scholastic laughter, but nothing tinged with cruelty. This was what Aristotle had called *eutrapelia*, the civilized laughter of joyful conversation without mockery or contempt. A later compromise is well illustrated in the Catholic festive carnival season followed by the abstemious period of Lent: first the eating, drinking and joking, then the serious business of denying oneself such pleasures.

In the 13th century, the highly religious King Louis IX of France is said to have found another convenient compromise, restricting his enjoyment of laughter but not entirely eliminating it: he would not allow himself to laugh on a Friday. Similar examples of an ambivalent attitude to humour in general and a particularly hostile attitude to comedians in particular were also seen in England, as recounted by Joseph Strutt in his 1801 book *The Sports and Pastimes of the People of England from the Earliest Period*. Strutt, we should point out, was perhaps not the most objective critic of such matters, as he makes clear when commenting on a passage from Philip Stubbes's *Anatomie of Abuses* (printed in 1583) that was highly critical of actors playing the part of "A Foole or a Vice" in dramatic performances. In Strutt's words: "Even when regular tragedies and comedies were introduced upon the stage, we may trace the descendants of this facetious Iniquity in the clowns and the fools which so frequently disgraced them." He then goes on to disparage the minstrels and jesters of the time (from which we may, incidentally, conclude that those whom the critics seek to disparage, they first misspell):

> The gestours, whose powers were chiefly employed in
> the hours of conviviality, finding by experience that
> lessons of instruction were much less seasonable at such
> times, than idle tales productive of mirth and laughter,
> accommodated their narrations to the general taste of
> the times, regardless of the mischiefs they occasioned by
> vitiating the morals of their hearers.

Warming to the topic, he had even worse to say about the minstrels:

> The extensive privileges enjoyed by the minstrels, and
> the long continuance of the public favour, inflated their
> pride and made them insolent; they even went so far as
> to claim their reward by a prescriptive right, and settled
> its amount according to the estimation they had formed
> of their own abilities, and the opulence of the noblemen
> into whose houses they thought proper to intrude.
> The large gratuities collected by these artists not only
> occasioned great numbers to join their fraternity, but also
> induced many idle and dissipated persons to assume the
> characters of minstrels, to the disgrace of the profession.
> These evils became at last so notorious, that in the reign
> of King Edward II it was thought necessary to restrain
> them by a public edict, which sufficiently explains the
> nature of the grievance.

Strutt does, however, think that there should be limits to the punishment deserved by minstrels and jesters for their impudence, as in the following case he recounts:

> It was, on the other hand, a very dangerous employment to censure the characters of great personages, or hold their actions up to ridicule; for, though the satirist might be secure at the moment, he was uncertain that fortune would not one day or another put him into the power of his adversary, which was the case with Luke de Barra, a celebrated Norman minstrel; who, in his songs having made very free with the character of Henry I of England, by some untoward accident fell into the hands of the irritated monarch. He condemned him to have his eyes pulled out: and, when the Earl of Flanders, who was present, pleaded warmly in his favour, the king replied: "This man, being a wit, a poet, and a minstrel, composed many indecent songs against me, and sung them openly to the great entertainment of mine enemies; and, since it has pleased God to deliver him into my hands, I will punish him, to deter others from the like petulance." The cruel sentence was executed, and the miserable satirist died soon after with the wounds he had received in struggling with the executioner.

Strutt then commented: "The gratification of a mean revenge is a strong mark of a little mind; and this inhumanity reflects great discredit upon the king: it would have been noble in him to have pardoned the unfortunate culprit."

Not until the second half of the 19th century did comedy start to gain general approval as variety theatre and music halls began to appear in Europe and Vaudeville began in the United States and Canada, and comedians started to become almost respectable, a theme we shall return to in the next chapter.

9
THEATRE

"There is a strange pecking order among actors. Theatre actors look down on film actors, who look down on TV actors. Thank God for reality shows, or we wouldn't have anybody to look down on."

George Clooney

I used to earn my living making trap doors in theatres. It was just a stage I was going through …

Humour may have been with us since the dawn of human evolution, but comedy as entertainment began in theatres in Greece in the sixth century BC. This is hardly surprising: ancient Greece led the world in cultural events – and radio, television and movies were still very far in the future – so where else could an entertainer hope to ply his trade? As we shall see, however, it took a long time for Greek comedy to develop into something we would recognize by the same name today.

Our word "comedy" in fact derives from the Greek *komoidia*, which comes from two words meaning "party" and "song", suggesting that dramatic comedy grew out of after-dinner banqueting hall entertainment, which moved into theatres in order to entertain many more. Aristotle, writing in the fourth century BC, suggested that comedy theatre began in festivals and phallic rituals, which could be seen as another form of after-dinner entertainment. For all the ancient Greeks, however, all that was required of a *komoidia* was a happy ending.

Its beginnings were seen in a festival called the City Dionysia, which celebrated Dionysus, god of fruitfulness, wine and ecstasy.

This had long included a competition between playwrights who each presented three tragedies and a more light-hearted play featuring rowdy mythological woodland spirits. These "satyr plays", as they were called, apparently became very popular. Around 486 BC, a third competition genre called *agon* (meaning conflict) was added to tragedy and satyr plays, out of which Old Comedy, as it was later called, grew. The *agon* took the form of a contest between two characters arguing about some issue. In many respects, particularly its ending in resolution and a happy ending, an a*gon* was similar to a satyr play but set in the real world without the mythological wood spirits.

The leading writer of the early *agon* plays, and thus perhaps the man most deserving of the title of first comic playwright, was Epicharmus, who lived for most of his long life in Syracuse where he wrote between 35 and 52 comic plays. Sadly almost all of these have been lost or preserved only in brief extracts, but he is known to have written one play called *The Sausage*. Although at times he received great praise, he also attracted frequent criticism for showing disrespect to the authorities or to mythical heroes.

This was the era which later became associated with the phase of Old Comedy – of which the undoubted master was Aristophanes. Its formats and stage techniques were much the same as those of tragedy, but what characterized it was the use of language for personal ridicule and satire. While only 11 of Aristophanes's 40 plays survive, we know of many of his lost plays from the criticism and praise they attracted. These both resulted from his plays' witty criticisms and merciless insults of those in political power. In his later works, however, Aristophanes relied to a lesser extent on crudeness and buffoonery, perhaps indicating that the Greek audiences were tiring of such things.

The rather vicious personal nature of Old Comedy gradually lessened until the end of the fifth century BC, when it gave way to Middle Comedy – of which very little has survived. We do, however, know that Middle Comedy dispensed with a chorus and frequent insults of specific politicians and consisted more of comment and general criticism not directed at specific individuals. Parasites, courtesans and, for some reason, conceited cooks were often targeted for criticism.

Around the middle of the fourth century BC, Middle Comedy gave way to New Comedy, which introduced fresh characters in the form of angry old men, compulsive parents and stupid but conceited mercenary soldiers. It also often featured a theme of love and romance which had been absent from Old and Middle Comedies.

The leading exponent of New Comedy was the Greek dramatist Menander, who wrote 108 comedies which won at least eight first prizes at Athens festival competitions. His plays remained popular until the Middle Ages but were lost between the 12th and 20th centuries before fragments were rediscovered around 1907.

The Greek influence in European culture, however, had been diminishing since 404 BC when Athens was finally defeated by the Spartans in the drawn-out Peloponnesian Wars. Although comedy continued, its development stagnated and the leadership of comedy theatre slowly shifted to Rome. The most highly acclaimed plays in the years early in the second century BC were those written by Plautus and Terence, both of whom took their themes from earlier Greek works. Plautus is generally admired for his humour, Terence for his characterization and insights into human nature.

One interesting feature of the manner in which Greek comedies were adapted for Roman audiences was the general tendency to maintain their settings in Greece, usually Athens itself. For the Greeks, this had the function of providing familiarity and increasing a sense of involvement for the audience, but for the Romans it gave the opportunity to disparage the Greeks and aspects of their society that the Romans considered primitive or undisciplined.

European comic dramatists followed the Greek and Roman formulae for comedy for more than a thousand years during the Middle Ages, when the influence of the Church reduced the joyous ambitions of comedy and sought to stifle its critical role. Once again, theatrical comedy was restricted to festivals and folk plays such as the medieval mummers' performances in England at Christmas or carnival performances in Germany and Austria. The development of comedy only resumed in Europe with the arrival of the Renaissance marking a rebirth of science, art and culture in the 16th century.

As far as comedy was concerned, the first confident steps were taken in Italy with the creation and growth of the commedia dell'arte, which rediscovered improvisation and brought us street theatre, Punch and Judy and pantomime, which came from the commedia character Harlequin.

While this liberalization was gathering pace in Europe, England was ruled by Elizabeth I and the royal court had throughout supported the growth of theatre, including comedy. The result had been entertainment that was enjoyed and appreciated by all classes, which increased public support for the monarchy and led to a golden age of theatrical comedies by playwrights such as Shakespeare and Ben Jonson.

In 1603, however, the Queen's health deteriorated and she was confined to her bedchamber at Richmond Palace. All public theatre performances were then banned until further notice and when Elizabeth died, theatres stayed closed as the nation mourned. A messenger was sent by horse to Edinburgh to inform King James VI of Scotland that he was now also James I of England under the English laws of succession.

Those involved in the theatre – including Shakespeare's own company, the Lord Chamberlain's Men – were concerned as they knew little about the new king, but they were delighted when James I announced that he would allow them to resume performances. Moreover, James himself would become sole sponsor of Shakespeare's company, which would now be known as the King's Men. Far from having their activities restricted, they would be allowed, according to the letters patent under the Great Seal dated 19 May 1603:

freely to use and exercise the art and faculty of playing comedies, tragedies, histories, and interludes, morals, pastorals, stage plays and such like as they have already studied or hereafter shall use or study, as well for the recreation of our loving subjects, as for our solace and pleasure when we shall think good to see them during our pleasure.

They would even appear at James's coronation, for which they were given a grant with which to buy scarlet cloth. Cautious at first, Shakespeare modified some of his earlier plays to take out anything that might be seen as insulting to Scotland and he was careful not to include anything that King James might find offensive. That, of course, applied mainly to his histories, but his comedies continued with the same innovations as he had already introduced. His characters were deeper and better drawn than those that earlier comic playwrights had managed to create and his romances always ended in weddings after the lovers had overcome various obstacles. Other writers adopted similar plots, but Shakespeare increased the complexity of his stories and emphasized the development of human relationship and their problems, which increased the audience's concerns and, most importantly, their ability to identify with the characters on the stage.

In some ways, Shakespeare's comedies stand up well today, but by modern standards the Bard too often repeats his use of easy comic devices such as shipwrecks that lead to separation, gender mix-up, disguise or identical twins leading to confusion, and deception for the sake of playing a trick on someone. Such things, however, were mostly new to his audiences and their repetition gave an increasing familiarity that must have been welcomed by fans. To add to the difficulty of assessing Shakespeare's contribution to the genre of comedy, however, is the fact that comedy, as we understand it today, was still not really considered a genre at the time.

The ancient Greeks, as we have already mentioned, applied the word "comedy" to any play with a happy ending. Making the audience laugh on the way to that ending was an optional extra. That was the reason behind the title of Dante's *Divine Comedy*: most of it was a thoroughly depressing trip through hell, but it had a happy ending in heaven and was therefore a comedy. However, one of Shakespeare's earliest plays, *The Comedy of Errors*, did have the intention of making his audience laugh and of all his comedies it is perhaps the only one that embraces laughter as its main if not only purpose. The plot was clearly taken from, or at least strongly influenced by, *The Menaechmi* which was written by Plautus around 200 BC and also featured mistaken identity and a pair of identical twins.

Significantly, Shakespeare did not himself categorize his plays as tragedies, histories and comedies, but those descriptions were applied by the early publishers who brought out collections of his works. Such descriptions, however, were rather inconsistent. *Troilus and Cressida*, for example, was described as a history in a 1609 Quarto edition, a comedy when it was reissued and finally a tragedy in the First Folio in 1623.

One of Shakespeare's greatest innovations, in fact, was to blur the boundaries between comedy and tragedy. Some of his comedies told basically tragic tales, while his tragedies more often than not included comic interludes. Such techniques, however, were not always appreciated by literary critics. In his essay "The Art, Rise and Progress of the Stage in Greece, Rome and England", published in 1710, the English writer Charles Gildon had this to say about the Bard:

> Grief and Laughter are so very incompatible, that to join these two Copies of Nature together, wou'd be monstrous and shocking to any Judicious Eye and yet this Absurdity is what is done so commonly among us in our Tragi-Comedies; this is what our Shakespear himself has frequently been guilty of, not only in those Mixtures which he has given us of that kind, but in many other Particulars for want of a thorough Knowledge of the Art of the Stage.

That at least gives us one possible answer to the thorny issue of why Shakespeare's comedies are not very funny: Charles Gildon would no doubt have believed it was because of Shakespeare's want of "a thorough Knowledge of the Art of the Stage". Yet one might argue that a less thorough knowledge of the art of the stage, or at least the history of that art, might have stopped Shakespeare pilfering plots from Plautus, which could have made his *Comedy of Errors* less ridiculous.

It was precisely because Shakespeare knew his art so well and what his audiences expected that he relied so heavily on tried and tested ways of getting laughs. Mistaken identities, misunderstandings, identical twins, enforced separations, joyful reunions and marriage were the standard formulas he relied on far too much, but they were the key to a successful comedy. Indeed, the one thing all Shakespearean comedies have in common is that they end with at least one marriage. Both *A Midsummer Night's Dream* and *Twelfth Night* have three marriages at the end and *As You Like It* sets the record at four. Not funny enough? Just add a marriage! In Shakespeare's time, of course, there was another aspect of one of his common plot devices that added to the humour: when a girl is disguised as a man, we should remember that all the girls' parts were played by men anyway, so it isn't really a girl disguised as a man but a man dressing up as a girl dressed up as a man. Oh, how they must have laughed!

Meanwhile, Shakespeare's tragedies have more than their fair share of jokesters: *Othello* and *Titus Andronicus* both have clowns, *Timon of Athens* has a fool, *Hamlet* has the jester Yorick – or at least his skull, with the gravediggers getting all the laughs, while *Cymbeline* hardly needs a jester when the king has a stepson as stupid as Cloten.

Perhaps this was Shakespeare's great comic contribution: the popularization of tragicomedy, yet Charles Gildon was not the only one to object to it: England's first Poet Laureate, John Dryden, was just as scathing: "There is no Theatre in the world has any thing so absurd as the English Tragi-comedie, 'tis a

Drama of our own invention, and the fashion of it is enough to proclaim it so; here a course of mirth, there another of sadness and passion; a third of honour, and fourth a Duel."

As Shakespeare knew, however, that's the formula for a tragedy; change the duel into a marriage, however, and you have a comedy. Curiously that is exactly the recipe that operas followed with great success throughout the 18th and 19th centuries. As George Bernard Shaw is said to have pointed out: "Opera is when a tenor and soprano want to make love, but are prevented from doing so by a baritone." This line has often been quoted, though nobody seems to give a source. If Shaw did say it, however, he was not quite right: the baritone is sometimes a bass, but with a little more thought, he would have realized that his comment could be expanded to give the difference between Grand Opera and Comic Opera: in Grand Opera the soprano dies; in Comic Opera, the tenor gets his girl and they live happily ever after.

It is, of course, highly unfair to criticize Shakespeare because his comedies are not funny, as humour, society and language have moved on in the past four hundred years and we would need a great deal of study to be able to put the Bard's writings in a proper historical context. Even National Theatre director Sir Richard Eyre, however, surprised his audience in a talk at a history festival in 2015, when he said: "a lot of Shakespeare's jokes aren't very good."

Around Shakespeare's time, however, and for many years after, the most privileged professional comedians were not singers or actors but the jesters who exhibited their skills at royal courts. In England, both James I and Charles I employed a jester named Archie Armstrong who had entertained James when he ruled Scotland and was officially elevated to court jester when James succeeded to the English throne. Armstrong was then paid an annual salary of £9 2s 6d (which was a little above the average wage at the time which was below £9) and later a pension of two shillings a day. Armstrong retained his post and his role as king's favourite when Charles I became the monarch, but his increasing rudeness to other courtiers showed a growing conceit and when he insulted the Archbishop of Canterbury, William Laud, in 1637, he had gone too far and was dismissed. By then, however, he had made a small fortune from a monopoly granted to him by James I in the manufacture of clay pipes, which allowed him to retire in comfort to an estate in the north of England where he lived for another 35 years.

The last official court jester in England was a man named Muckle John who kept a remarkably low profile when he served Charles I and lost his job when the king was beheaded in 1649. The rulers of Poland, France and Heidelberg also had court jesters between the 16th and 18th centuries, and Henrietta Maria of France was the last to have a court dwarf, but perhaps the most remarkable appointment to such a role was that of Jesse Bogdanoff, who became jester to King Tupoi IV of Tonga in 1999.

Bogdanoff was a Bank of America financial adviser who made a good deal of money for Tonga, which he planned to promote as a tourist destination. His qualifications for the job of court jester were rather unclear, though he did point out that his birthday was April 1 and he did play the saxophone at royal events. After losing much Tongan money on speculative investments, however, he became persona non grata in that country in 2004 and returned to the US. According to a report in 2006, he then became a therapist using hypnosis to treat post-traumatic stress.

Meanwhile, back in England in the 17th century, the country's parliament suffered stresses of its own as it fell under the grip of religious fervour and the Puritanical rule of Oliver Cromwell. London's theatres were considered ungodly and were closed in 1642 and in 1647 a law was passed to punish anyone who participated in or viewed drama. Theatres remained silent until Charles II returned in 1660. Very soon after the restoration of the monarchy, however, the king ensured the restoration of theatres in general, and comedy in particular, and theatrical comedy took full advantage of this opportunity to reinvent itself.

Not only had the 18-year lay-off resulted in technical developments such as moveable scenery, footlights and more elaborate stage and theatre design, but for the first time theatre companies were permitted and even encouraged to allow female parts to be played by women.

As the middle classes flourished and grew, more people became attracted to nights out at the theatre and theatre designers exploited this democratization of audiences by designing their buildings with lower-priced sections for the professional classes and lower prices still for the working class. Particularly when staging comedies, this often led to a rather raucous section of the audience in the gallery, which added to the gaiety and high-spirited atmosphere of the performances.

The Greeks and Romans had attracted audiences with a good deal of smut, while Shakespeare's comedies had been more refined, but the early years of Restoration comedy saw a conscious blend of these styles combining immorality with genuine wit and parody, particularly at the expense of the upper classes. Once again, however, this led to a backlash when royal support for the theatre came to an end after Charles II died in 1685, to be followed by three years of unrest when his brother James II succeeded him, resumed the old battles with parliament and was deposed in 1688. The following year William and Mary began their rule, which was bad news for the theatre, of which they generally disapproved.

This greatly encouraged the Puritans, who had always opposed both the theatre and comedy. In 1692, a Society for the Reformation of Manners was founded, one of whose prime objectives was to restore morality and decency to the stage. They were also actively opposed to brothels, prostitution and profanity but specifically brought lawsuits against playwrights whose works they saw as containing insufficient moral instruction.

The influential theologian and theatre critic Jeremy Collier certainly shared the views of the Society for the Reformation of Manners as far as comedy theatre was concerned, as he made clear in a pamphlet he published in 1698 with the pompous title *A Short View of the Immorality and Profaneness of the English Stage*. Referring to "Comedy's unruly voices of libertine disorder", he came out strongly against all Restoration comedy and was particularly critical of the works of Vanbrugh and Congreve, who had been the most brilliantly successful writers of the genre he so despised. "Comedy", Collier said, "required a profound rethink" and needed replacing by "good order in political and family life".

Unsurprisingly, this was also the period in which the first signs of stage censorship were seen. In 1696, the Lord Chamberlain, who was the most senior figure of the royal household, gave instructions to those overseeing the production of plays to be "very careful in correcting all obscenities and other scandalous matters and such as any ways offend against ye laws of God and good manners or the known statutes of the kingdom".

One aspect of good manners and immorality and profaneness and obscenities that is rarely mentioned in discussions of such matters, however, was raised in Michael Burden's paper, "Pots, privies and WCs: crapping at the opera in London before 1830", which appeared in the *Cambridge Opera Journal* in 2011. Remarking on the lack of toilet facilities in the early London theatre and the habit of theatre-goers of taking chamber pots with them, Burden draws attention to the lack of evidence of how and when these were used, pointing out that many performances went on for quite some time and did not have intervals. "Once the pots had been used", he points out, "their contents would have made the auditoria stink" and he quotes one report from 1830 which noted that "notwithstanding the liberal use of perfume by the ladies . . . the house retained some of the disagreeable odour left by the filthy mob that filled it on the previous night." Professor of Performing Arts Tracy C. Davis has pointed out that audiences had been bringing chamber pots to the theatre since the days of Imperial Rome, and "presumably they continued to do so, or just relieved themselves on the spot".

With uncontrolled audiences relieving themselves in such a manner, it is perhaps surprising that anyone bothered with the relatively mild stench of supposed immorality onstage, but perhaps that was a welcome distraction from the smell. Whatever the reason, statutory censorship was introduced in the Licensing Act 1737, which gave the Lord Chamberlain the right to veto performances of new plays or modifications to old plays. This was largely done as a way of limiting political satire against Robert Walpole's government and it was still some 18 years before the phrase "water-closet" entered the language and much longer, of course, before proper plumbing and WCs were installed in London's theatres.

The Licensing Act remained law for the next 230 years, with all scripts for public performance having to be submitted to the Lord Chamberlain's office. They were then scrutinized and unacceptable words, jokes or actions in the script were underlined in blue pencil and had to be removed. There is a theory that this was why we have the expressions "blue joke" and "blue movie", but the *Oxford English Dictionary* just tells us that the origin of such expressions is "uncertain".

Blue pencil or not, the Lord Chamberlain's powers were slightly lessened in Britain by the Theatrical Representations Act of 1788, which allowed local magistrates to authorize performances for up to 60 days. Then the Theatres Act of 1843 diminished them further, limiting the Lord Chamberlain's powers to prohibit performances to cases in which "it is fitting for the preservation of good manners, decorum or of the public peace so to do". Finally, censorship was abolished by the 1968 Theatres Act; in some cases it had in any case become pointless as theatres had got round the regulations by turning themselves into private members' clubs.

Partly because of the fear of censorship, but also because changes in society influenced the audiences, the popularity of theatrical comedy in Britain went through several different phases in the 18th and 19th centuries. First, the continuing reaction against frivolity and bawdiness led to a more sentimental type of comedy, which proved to be less outrageous and, perhaps because of that, less popular.

The Irish playwright and politician Richard Brinsley Sheridan brought back satire and wit in works such as *The Rivals* and *The School for Scandal*, which caused a brief revival of comedy in the 1770s, but the early 19th century saw another slump until a revival of interest in wit was inspired by writers such as Oscar Wilde and George Bernard Shaw.

From the mid-19th century onwards, however, society was moving at a faster pace than the theatre could keep up with. The industrial revolution in Europe and the American Civil War changed expectations for everyone and created a thirst for new types of undemanding variety entertainment for all. In France, this was supplied by a theatrical genre called vaudeville, with the Americans using the same word to describe their own very different brand of variety shows, while in England the same societal demands resulted in the establishment of music halls. A major factor in the popularity of all of these was comedy.

Vaudeville probably took its name from the Vau de Vire (the Vire Valley in Calvados, Normandy) where a 15th-century group called Companions of the Vau de Vire wrote drinking songs to well-known tunes (though another view is that the name comes from the more general term Voix de Ville, meaning Voice of the City). What started as drinking songs, however, grew into a highly successful theatrical entertainment that gave the Parisian public exactly what it wanted: an undemanding night's entertainment to round off a day in the capital. Unlike the American entertainment of the same name or British music hall, the Parisian vaudeville was not a variety show but combined music and humour in a one-act play.

With early trains and buses making travel easier, and shops and restaurants increasing quickly in number in central Paris, a new consumer culture was growing and bringing fresh audiences to the many theatres that were now springing up. Traditionally, plays in theatres had tended to carry a moral message or at least have a worthy theme, but that was not what the new, middle-class theatre-goer wanted. Instead, the typical vaudeville productions combined music and comedy in a formulaic manner with satire, actors' gestures, stage props and word games all playing their parts in keeping the audience amused. In earlier times, the music had been the most important part but in vaudeville the plots, action and dialogue came to the fore, as the heroes, usually a pair of lovers, were threatened with disaster from which they ultimately escaped in an unlikely manner. As US literature professor Jennifer Terni summarized it in 2006, vaudeville was "a protracted foray into disaster control". The ending was predictable, but how they arrived there was always a surprise, and that is what the public loved.

At its peak around 1850, vaudeville theatres in Paris are estimated to have taken more than half of all box office receipts in that period, attracting between two-and-a-half and three million spectators every year. Well over half the new plays shown in Paris were vaudeville comedies. More than ever before, the people going to the theatre could see themselves in the roles portrayed on stage. The characters who stood for tradition were depicted in a negative manner and vaudeville played its part in progressing from the old order to modernity. And there was always a happy ending.

French vaudeville itself may also be seen to have had a happy ending. Its popularity certainly faded rapidly with the advent of talking cinema, but the style of music and comedy it brought had led to the development of *opéra-comique* in France and *opera buffa* in Italy. The formulaic style of its humour, without the music, may also be seen as a clear precursor of modern TV sitcoms.

The development of 19th-century comedy in America was in many ways similar to the French experience, but what they called vaudeville in the US was more an attempt to cash in on the reputation and success of the French version than an attempt to copy it. The genres were linked by a common realization that a blend of music and comedy was what people wanted; however, the French achieved this in the form of a short play while the Americans preferred a number of fast, unrelated variety acts. As well as the comedians and singers, there were jugglers, magicians, dancers and even trained animal acts.

Variety theatre had become popular in the United States in the mid-19th century, originating in beer halls where the audiences were mainly men and the comedy ranged from the rather coarse to the totally obscene. Out of this grew American vaudeville, which set out to be clean, wholesome family entertainment and in which the comedy element proved especially popular. Vaudeville brought a great deal of business to theatres, attracting audiences that included women and children, and from the late 1890s onwards, many shows began to include short motion pictures in their performances. By the time the talkies arrived in 1927, it was becoming increasingly clear that movies were going to drive vaudeville acts out of business and the depression of the 1930s hastened the process.

In Britain, the fate of the music hall followed a very similar progression, although it lasted for longer. Music hall's precursors were various venues ranging from coffee houses and taverns that introduced entertainment to lure in customers, to theatres that had transformed themselves officially into members-only clubs in order to get round the censorship restrictions imposed by the Theatres Act. As in America, these venues at first attracted mainly male audiences, but as in both America and France, the proprietors and producers soon discovered that family entertainment proved to be more popular.

Many of the venues grew into grand theatres to accommodate larger audiences, often of over 1,000 people. By the mid-1870s there were nearly 400 music halls in London alone, with a similar number around the rest of the country, and each of these required its own comedians. This brought two obvious advantages to the performers: first, there were more jobs for comedians than ever before, and second, after appearing at one venue, they could take the same act to another without changing a word as they were reaching a totally different audience.

The managers of the music halls tried to introduce exclusivity contracts for performers, which led to frequent disputes. The comedians also had another battle to fight, as the humour became more risqué, the theatres more bawdy and the London

County Council imposed more restrictions, including the issuing of liquor licences. Audiences began to decrease, which some said was due to the unavailability of alcohol, and revenues were threatened.

This led, in 1907, to a strike by performers, starting at the Holborn Empire and then spreading to other venues. Marie Lloyd, whose songs, full of innuendo and double entendres, had made her one of music hall's great stars, performed in front of crowds on the picket line, explaining her reasons for striking: "We the stars can dictate our own terms. We are fighting not for ourselves, but for the poorer members of the profession, earning thirty shillings to £3 a week." The management, she pointed out, were increasing their work load with extra matinée performances and extra variety slots without increasing their pay.

After two weeks, the management backed down, but the great days of the music hall were almost over. The First World War was on its way; entertainment in general, and comedy in particular, were about to face fresh opportunities and challenges with the advent of radio, film and television. While these were developing, however, a new brand of popular comedy theatre emerged, which filled the growing need for escapism in an era of increasing international tension.

The new genre, which became known as farce, was created by French playwright Georges Feydeau in the 1880s and according to contemporary critics produced more laughter in Parisian theatres than had ever been heard before. Feydeau, incidentally, was a depressive, compulsive gambler and syphilitic, which resulted in severe mental illness that ended with his spending his last two years in a sanatorium, where he issued invitations to his coronation as he thought that he was Napoleon III. Whatever his own state of mind, however, he certainly knew what made other people laugh.

Feydeau himself never called his plays "farces" but referred to them as *comédies* or *vaudevilles*, which reflected their origins in French vaudeville theatre, as the *Oxford English Dictionary* explains in its fascinating account of the history of the word "farce".

The word originally appeared in both English and French in the 13th century from ecclesiastical Latin, where the term *farsa* or *farsia* was used to describe various phrases interpolated in litanies. The use of *farce* thus came to be expanded to mean any filling out, from forcemeat stuffing used in cookery to the spontaneous buffoonery interpolated by actors in religious dramas. The last of these meanings was then applied to comic interludes spoken by vaudeville performers between their songs in Parisian theatres and finally as a specific brand of comic theatre or derogatory term for real-life political ludicrousness.

Whatever he may have called them, Georges Feydeau wrote over 20 full-length farces and almost the same number again of one-act plays between 1886 and 1914. His formula for the three-act farces was invariable and highly successful: the first act introduced the characters and the situation in which they found themselves; the second act saw the situations develop in a frenzied style; the third act was devoted to sorting things out and getting everything back to normal.

As Feydeau said, his task as a writer was to identify characters who have every reason to avoid each other, then bring them together as soon and as often as possible. His style was to place ordinary people in dramatic situations, then observe them from a comic angle, "but they must never be allowed to say or do anything which is not strictly demanded, first by their character and secondly by the plot". In addition, and perhaps most surprising of all, he avowedly avoided wit in his scripts, believing strongly that witty dialogue interrupted the action.

Despite the success of Feydeau's unpretentiously funny farces, the genre was slow to be adopted in England but proved to be just the light relief the nation needed after the First World War and again after the Second. From 1923 to 1933, London's Aldwych Theatre was home to a dozen farces, most of which were written by Ben Travers. The style featured similar lunacy to that of Feydeau, but also incorporated witty dialogue which seemed more to the taste of the British.

Many of these farces were also performed around Britain by touring companies and several of them became films performed by members of the original stage cast. With the actors increasingly involved in these cinema productions and Travers himself involved in writing the screenplays, the Aldwych Theatre then moved on to stage other plays from 1933 onwards. The increasing seriousness of the international situation soon lessened the demand for farces and it was not long before the war put a stop to theatrical activity altogether.

In 1950, however, farces returned stronger than ever in a new venue at London's Whitehall Theatre. The production company, run by a young actor named Brian Rix, began with a perfectly chosen play called *Reluctant Heroes* by Colin Morris, about a drill sergeant having problems controlling his troops. It caught the mood of the nation perfectly, blending everyone's shared wartime experiences with the need for laughter. This ran for four years and more than 1,600 performances and was also shown on television, which actually increased the number of people wanting to see it on stage. Despite generally being panned by po-faced critics, it was loved by the audiences.

Reluctant Heroes was followed by John Chapman's *Dry Rot*, which also played for four years. On the day that the Whitehall farces had been running even longer that their predecessors at the Aldwych, Rix celebrated by offering a glass of champagne to everyone in the audience. In 1966, after 16 years of simple-minded, trouser-dropping hilarity at the Whitehall, the record-breaking run came to an end because the lease of the theatre came up for renewal and it was too expensive to do so.

Even though the audiences for farce diminished when it lost its home at the Whitehall, this brand of humour still retains many followers. In 1968, the abolition of theatre censorship in Britain tempted Ben Travers out of retirement by at last letting him refer to his favourite topic of sexual matters in his writing without innuendo or allusion. In 1975, in his 90th year, he saw his new play *The Bed Before Yesterday* produced on the London stage. Not only did it run for longer than any of his Aldwych farces almost 50 years earlier, but with two more of his farces celebrating revivals it was only one of a remarkable trio of Ben Travers works on stage in London at the same time.

"The way the world is, I think a silly evening in the theatre is a good thing, to take our minds off terror."

Tim Curry

10
CINEMA

"Life is a tragedy when seen in close-up, but a comedy in long-shot."

Charlie Chaplin

A man walks into a cinema and is astonished to see a pig wandering around. Disgusted by the sight, the man asks: "Why is there a pig in this cinema?"
The pig turns around and says, "I liked the book."

The advent of motion pictures around the start of the 20th century gave a great boost to comedy. Their novelty was highly attractive to the public and in the era of silent movies short comic films were the best way to attract audiences. One of the first demonstrations of the new technology was a 49-second film shown by Louis Lumière in 1895 originally called simply *Le Jardinier* ("the gardener") before its title was changed to *L'Arroseur Arrosé*, which was translated as *The Sprinkler Sprinkled* when it was shown in England. The plot was simple, featuring a boy playing a trick on a gardener who was watering his roses. The boy stopped the water flow by stepping on the hose, but when the gardener lifted the hose to inspect it, the boy lifted his foot, causing the water to spray in the poor fellow's face. Eventually, the gardener realized what was happening, chased and caught the boy, then delivered a spanking. And the audiences loved it. It is perhaps no coincidence that the word "slapstick" has its earliest citation in the *Oxford English Dictionary* listed as 1896, though the original meaning of the word was apparently descriptive of two flat pieces of wood joined together to make a slapping sound in pantomimes to accompany the scene of someone being thumped.

Slapstick comedy quickly played a major role in the success of silent movies. Originally many had thought that the main appeal of moving pictures would be in historical re-enactments or filmed events or items of interest in exotic locations, but it was comedy that proved most reliable in attracting large audiences and making the leading comic actors better known than ever before.

Perhaps the first true film star was French actor/director Max Linder, who made over 100 short films in the role he created as "Max", a wealthy, well-dressed man-about-town who always seemed to get into scrapes when pursuing his love of beautiful women. His fame spread throughout Europe where he became the highest-paid entertainer in the years leading up to the First World War. However, after the war, poor health, depression and an ill-advised move to America combined to cause a slump in Linder's fortunes and he was quickly replaced in the affections of audiences by a generation of great comics who truly understood how to bring out the best in the new techniques of silent movies.

On the plus side, films improved on theatre in three main ways: they facilitated various apparently impossible effects through trick photography and editing; scenes could be re-shot if they went wrong and only the best versions shown to the public; and the actors had to get things right only once and not restrict themselves to routines they could confidently perform without mistakes every night. The last of these let them perform far more roles than ever before, thus increasing their fame and their revenues.

On the other hand, the disadvantage of silent movies is clear from their all too honest title: they were silent, which not only severely restricted the type of material they could deliver, but also forced the actors to exaggerate their facial expressions to help convey their emotions, which audiences found unnatural. As early attempts failed to synchronize sound and action, the only means of verbal communication was through captions (technically known as title cards or intertitles) which occasionally interrupted the action to explain what was happening.

For these reasons, the silent film era of comedies concentrated almost exclusively on visual humour, such as Charlie Chaplin's characteristic moustache, twirling cane and silly walk, or Ben Turpin's cross-eyed appearance, or Roscoe "Fatty" Arbuckle's huge size, or the deadpan expression of Buster Keaton. Dangerous-looking stunts (which were often genuine rather than trick photography) also contributed to the appeal of their films. On one occasion, during a publicity shoot, an exploding bomb on set even cost one of the greatest silent film stars, Harold Lloyd, the thumb and index finger of his right hand. In subsequent movies, he wore a glove with a prosthetic rubber thumb and forefinger to cover up the injury.

All those named above became household names in the silent film era, but when the talkies arrived, most were unable to adapt their styles successfully. In some cases, this was because their voices were simply off-putting, but for others, the shift from visual to verbal humour was too great a challenge. One of the greatest success stories in moving from silent films to talkies, however, was that of the first great comedy duo, Laurel and Hardy.

First individually, then as a pair, they had had quite an illustrious career in silent films before talkies welcomed them. They made over 30 silent film shorts together before 1930, then went on to make 40 short and 23 full-length films as well as a number of stage appearances. Stan Laurel, the Englishman, and Oliver Hardy, the American, had both been successful comedians on their own but were perfect as a partnership. Ollie, huge and bombastic, was a pompous bully; Stan, thin and cowardly, was terrified of everything the world had to offer, and both men brought a range of visual ideas they had learned from silent films into the world of talkies, turning them into familiar gestures and self-conscious mannerisms which complemented a repertoire of catchphrases that the public adored. Stan, who early in his career had served as Charlie Chaplin's understudy, would burst into tears and pull his hair upwards when frightened, while Ollie, who had been a singer at the start of his career, was always liable to accuse Stan with the words: "Well, here's another nice mess you've gotten me into." It was probably the most recognizable catchphrase of its time.

In the two decades between the world wars, the only comic acts that could rival Laurel and Hardy's success in films were those of W. C. Fields and Harold Lloyd, also survivors who had very successfully adapted from the silent era, followed slightly later by the Marx Brothers and the Three Stooges. Their styles of comedy were very different, but all perfectly supplied aspects of the escapism that the public wanted in the difficult interwar period.

Harold Lloyd was perhaps the most versatile of these, generally portraying a likeable young man, modest, but with confidence and ambition. Although the roles he played were varied, he was instantly recognizable for his unpretentious horn-rimmed glasses. He didn't need glasses, but they went perfectly with his boy-next-door image. He wore them with the lenses removed and they became his most identifiable feature, earning considerable praise from opticians who praised him as "the man who popularized eye-glasses in America". His first pair cost him 75 cents and brought an added bonus: "With them, I am Harold Lloyd; without them, a private citizen," he explained. "I can stroll unrecognized down any street in the land at any time without the glasses, a boon granted no other picture actor and one which some of them would pay well for."

In the silent movies, Lloyd had earned a reputation for hair-raising stunts, including his most famous scene, hanging off the hands of a town clock high above the street in *Safety Last!* This was a trick shot, of course, but very effective and even if people didn't know his name, they knew who you were talking about when you referred to "the man on the clock".

In the 1920s, Lloyd was probably the highest-paid actor in films, but his reputation went even higher when dialogue became possible. This gave him the opportunity to develop and deepen his likeable everyman persona, which made it even easier for the audience to identify with him. Admittedly, this became less realistic during the Depression years of the 1930s, and the popularity of his films dropped a little, but by then he had his own film company and had built a 44-room mansion in Beverley Hills. In 1953, he was given an honorary Academy Award for being "a master comedian and good citizen".

Just as Harold Lloyd had appealed to the well-motivated, decent side of the American character, both W. C. Fields and the Three Stooges took the other extreme, sticking to the slapstick character of the silent era. Fields, who had started his career as a vaudeville juggler, added comedy to his act and then gave up the juggling. Finally, he developed the role that made him famous: an unpleasant, belligerent alcoholic who hated dogs and children, and who spoke with an arrogant drawl. This was surprisingly well received by audiences, in much the same way that they had loved booing at villains in Victorian melodrama and silent films. His acting did not so much bring out the worst in those who saw it, as reassure them that they were not so bad anyway. They also laughed at his depiction of such awfulness. Perhaps after the horrors of the Great War, it was good to see something terrible that they could laugh at, and such characters even lightened the impact of the Depression in their portrayal of workers (or idlers) fighting a class struggle.

The Three Stooges also got their laughs from acts of ill will and violence toward each other, but in a way that continued the slapstick tradition as their peculiar mixture of aggression and cowardice led them into trouble. Indeed, much of the conversation between them consisted of abuse, expressions of anger or Yiddish slang terms which most of the audience would not understand. Charlie Chaplin and Buster Keaton may have specialized in portraying innocent downtrodden people with whom the audience could identify, but the Three Stooges – Larry, Moe and Shemp (later replaced by Curly) – were anything but innocent and generally deserved all the custard pies thrown at them. And then the Marx Brothers arrived, with a virtuoso display of comedy the likes of which had never been seen before.

Julius, Leonard and Adolph Marx (and occasionally Herbert), who became known to all as Groucho, Chico and Harpo (and occasionally Zeppo), brought a brilliant new style of comedy to cinemas in the 1930s. Their parents were Jewish immigrants who emigrated around 1880 to New York where both made a living as entertainers. Their mother yodelled and played the harp, and their father was a ventriloquist, so it was natural that the brothers went into vaudeville as a musical troupe. Their act began as music with a little comedy, but soon became comedy with a little music and before long their stage personae began to develop: Groucho as the fast-talking, wisecracking head of the group, Chico with a mock Italian accent, and Harpo as the harp-playing brother who never spoke, the reason for which is typically extraordinary.

Before 1914, they had been on tour performing a show called *Home Again* in which, as was usual at that time, Harpo had a small speaking part. Al Shean, the producer of that show, who was also their uncle and manager, had only given Harpo a few lines, as he thought Harpo's voice was unpleasant, but in one performance in the town of Champaign, Illinois, Harpo decided to ad lib extra dialogue for himself. He was hurt when he read a review in a local newspaper soon after which said: "Adolph Marx performed beautiful pantomime which was ruined whenever he spoke", and so Adolph, even before he adopted the name Harpo, vowed never again to speak on stage. Instead, he developed the character of a mute, who communicated with gestures, whistles or honks of a horn, and the audience loved it.

Harpo's extraordinary act, combined with Chico's ludicrous mock-Italian accent and Groucho's speed of delivery, fake moustache and stooping walk, broke all the rules and brought a new era of comedy to the cinema. Other full-length film comedies had plausible plots, usually romantic, with occasionally amusing dialogue and happy endings; the Marx Brothers films were pure comedy from start to finish, with superb dialogue written by a new generation of script writers such as George Kaufman and

Bert Kalmar (who collaborated on *Animal Crackers*) and perhaps most brilliant of all, S. J. Perelman (who wrote both *Monkey Business* and *Horse Feathers*), but their real genius was in knowing the sort of lines that Groucho would deliver most effectively in his unique manner. Here are a dozen of my favourites. There is no way of knowing for sure which were scripted for Groucho and which were created by the man himself but they all have the characteristic Marx Brothers irreverence:

1. Outside of a dog, a book is man's best friend. Inside of a dog, it's too dark to read.
2. I find television very educating. Every time somebody turns on the set, I go into the other room and read a book.
3. Those are my principles. If you don't like them, I have others.
4. Women should be obscene and not heard.
5. I never forget a face, but in your case, I'll be glad to make an exception.
6. I could dance with you till the cows come home, on second thought I'll dance with the cows till you come home.
7. Marriage is a wonderful institution, but who wants to live in an institution?
8. Why, I'd horse-whip you if I had a horse.
9. The secret of life is honesty and fair dealing. If you can fake that, you've got it made.
10. I'm not crazy about reality, but it's still the only place to get a decent meal.
11. While money can't buy happiness, it certainly lets you choose your own form of misery.
12. Just give me a comfortable couch, a dog, a good book, and a woman. Then if you can get the dog to go somewhere and read the book, I might have a little fun.

And finally, here is something from *Animal Crackers* which was most probably written by S. J. Perelman, but needs to be read in the fast-talking, nonchalant Groucho manner to achieve the best effect: "Well, we must remember that art is art, isn't it? Though, on the other hand, water is water! And east is east and west is west and if you take cranberries and stew them like applesauce they taste much more like prunes than rhubarb does. Now, uh . . . now you tell me what you know."

And post-ultimately, before we leave the Marx Brothers, let us remember that Groucho himself said "humour is reason gone mad", which is as astute a statement about humour as you will read in this or any other book on the subject.

The hugely successful film career of the Marx Brothers extended between 1930 and 1949, which by a curious coincidence was also the peak time for the strict and powerful brand of censorship in the movie industry known as the Hays Code. Will H. Hays was a minor US politician who had served as Postmaster General from 1920 to 1922 but was then elected as the first chairman of the Motion Picture Producers and Distributors of America, a post he would hold until 1945. At the time, the morality of the movie industry and its stars was coming under increasing criticism and state censorship boards had been set up to authorise the release of films, making cuts where they thought necessary. Seeing the formation of a federal censorship authority as part of his job, Hays set about the task of cleaning up the film industry, and that included comedies.

In 1921, a great scandal had hit America in the form of the arrest of "Fatty" Arbuckle for the rape and manslaughter of actress Virginia Rappe. At the time, Arbuckle was probably the second most successful and highly paid film comedian behind Charlie Chaplin and his trial caused a sensation. The prosecution even claimed, without bringing any evidence to support it, that the actress had been crushed by Arbuckle's massive weight. The jury would not budge from voting 10 to 2 in favour of acquittal, and a retrial was ordered, which also ended 10 to 2, but this time in favour of conviction, probably because the defence was so convinced they would win that they did not present their case. At the third trial, however, in April 1922, the jury took only six minutes to return a not guilty verdict and the foreman even presented an apology: "Acquittal is not enough for Roscoe Arbuckle. We feel that a great injustice has been done him. We feel also that it was only our plain duty to give him this exoneration, under the evidence, for there was not the slightest proof adduced to connect him in any way with the commission of a crime."

Despite this, Arbuckle's career was over. Will H. Hays's first act as head of the MPPDA, which took place after the acquittal, was to cancel all bookings of "Fatty" Arbuckle films in the United States of America. That decision was never rescinded.

Despite Hays's obvious power conveyed by this story, it took him a long time to achieve success in his ambition of creating effective federal censorship. Even when he did produce a Motion Pictures Production Code in 1931, it was often ignored and took another three years before it began to have a strong effect, thanks to support from an even more conservative group which called itself the National League of Decency.

Nowadays, such a name might conjure up visions of a band of superheroes dedicated to protecting the moral virtues of the nation, which was precisely how the National League of Decency saw themselves.

Formed in 1934, they began as a loose union of Catholic churches whose members pledged to patronize only those motion pictures which did not "offend decency and Christian morality" and acknowledged their "obligation to form a right conscience about pictures that are dangerous to my moral life". These were the noble objectives that gained the National League of Decency the effective leadership of the growing campaign against immorality, particularly in movies, and they thoroughly approved of and supported the Motion Pictures Production Code, which by then was generally known as the Hays Code. The Code began with three General Principles:

1. No picture shall be produced which will lower the moral standards of those who see it. Hence the sympathy of the

audience shall never be thrown to the side of crime, wrong-doing, evil or sin.

2. Correct standards of life, subject only to the requirements of drama and entertainment, shall be presented.

3. Law, natural or human, shall not be ridiculed, nor shall sympathy be created for its violation.

There were around a dozen sections indicating areas such as murder, nudity and blasphemy that were forbidden by the Code, followed by another 20 or so about which caution should be exercised. "Bedroom scenes", it said, "must be treated with discretion." The Code itself did not specify, as has often been claimed, that in any scene depicting a man, a woman and a bed, the actors must each keep at least one foot on the floor; however, that was the way the rule was interpreted by most studios. For 20 years, married men and women in films were therefore always shown as sleeping in separate beds.

The Code was updated occasionally to keep pace with changes in morality or society. In the 1940s, for example, a sample list of forbidden words was added:

No approval by the Production Code Administration shall be given to the use of words and phrases in motion pictures including, but not limited to, the following:

Alley cat (applied to a woman); bat (applied to a woman); broad (applied to a woman); Bronx cheer (the sound); chippie; cocotte; God, Lord, Jesus, Christ (unless used reverently); cripes; fanny; fairy (in a vulgar sense); finger (the); fire, cries of; Gawd; goose (in a vulgar sense); "hold your hat" or "hats"; hot (applied to a woman); "in your hat"; louse; lousy; Madam (relating to prostitution); nance, nerts; nuts (except when meaning crazy); pansy; razzberry (the sound); slut (applied to a woman); SOB; son-of-a; tart; toilet gags; tom cat (applied to a man); traveling salesman and farmer's daughter jokes; whore;

damn; hell (excepting when the use of said last two words shall be essential and required for portrayal, in proper historical context, of any scene or dialogue based upon historical fact or folklore, or for the presentation in proper literary context of a Biblical, or other religious quotation, or a quotation from a literary work provided that no such use shall be permitted which is intrinsically objectionable or offends good taste).

As part of their campaign, the League of Decency even produced a rating system for films which was a forerunner of all later such systems adopted by America and other nations. They rated all films in one of the following categories: A: morally unobjectionable; B: Morally objectionable in part; or C: Condemned. Later, the A category was split into A-I (for general patronage) and A-II (adults and adolescents only); and later still A-III (adults only) and A-IV (adults but with some reservations) were added.

What, you may be asking, does all this have to do with comedy in general and the Marx Brothers in particular? On the one hand, their comedy was often outrageously anarchic and full of blatant sexual innuendo, so its contents clearly fell under the rules of the Code, but on the other hand, they were so crazy that nobody could possibly take them seriously.

In 2017, the comic writer and performer Donald Travis Stewart watched all the Marx Brothers films "for the zillionth time", as he put it, looking for differences between their pre-Code and post-Code antics. He knew that the later films were just as funny as the older ones, so he was not expecting to find much but was surprised at his conclusions, which he reported on his Travalanche website.

The matter is somewhat complicated by the fact that the Marx Brothers moved from Paramount Studios to MGM in 1935, so it is unclear whether any changes are due to the increased strictness of the Hays Code or a difference in the style of the studios, but Stewart certainly detected noticeable changes in the content of their films. Harpo's earlier tendency to chase women disappeared almost completely and larceny vanished from the characters of both Chico and Harpo. In the early films, both of them were habitual pickpockets, while Harpo's own voluminous pockets were always filled with a bewildering variety of objects, most of which he may be assumed to have purloined in a manner that could be judged as contravening the Code by glorifying crime or lowering the moral standards of those who saw it. Groucho's amorous activities are also curtailed and Stewart also identifies some definite examples of his innuendo-laden lines being cut. His article is headed by a photo of the Marx Brothers looking grumpy, with a caption saying: "*I sure wish these bean counters would let us be funny again!*"

Paradoxically, however, the Code also had the effect of forcing Hollywood to create new genres of comedy which proved to be very popular and successful in a nation that needed something light and relaxing in the years during and after the Depression. With overt adultery, seduction and sexual relations ruled out, new ways had to be found to suggest a growing relationship and compatibility between a man and a woman. The style of comedy that grew out of this was given a name that juxtaposed two terms that were just the sort of words the Hays Code might view with great suspicion: "screw" and "ball".

Screwball comedy used witty dialogue as a sexual substitute and portrayed slapstick antics as a sign of carelessness or eccentricity rather than violence; and although the word "screw" had been used in a sexual sense since at least the 18th century, "screwy" was increasingly the word of choice to describe something ridiculous or unexpected. The term "screwball" had originated in baseball and cricket but was now adopted as the favoured description of comedy films whose plots went in unexpected directions after being placed in unbelievable settings in the first place.

The optimism and unreality of such films made them an instant success. In 1934, the year in which the Hays Code became rigidly enforced, Clark Gable and Claudette Colbert starred in *It Happened One Night* and the film was a raging success. It was the first to win all five major Academy Awards: Best Film, Best Actor, Best Actress, Best Director and Best Adapted Screenplay, an achievement that has only been matched by two later films: *One Flew Over the Cuckoo's Nest* and *Silence of the Lambs*. The plot centred on an unlikely couple (she was an heiress running away from her family, he was a rebellious journalist) to whom unlikely things happened (they met on a bus which left them behind at a stop in the middle of nowhere) and unlikely consequences ensued: they fell in love – but the audience knew from the start that was what was going to happen.

The director Frank Capra, who had won all those Oscars for *It Happened One Night*, again won Best Picture and Best Director in 1938 for another screwball comedy, *You Can't Take It with You*, but the limitations of screwball comedy were already beginning to tire audiences. Their zaniness, double entendres and romances were becoming too predictable and comedy needed to find a new way forward. Fortunately, the comic actors, and perhaps even more importantly their scriptwriters, were fully up to the task. This time, just as the Depression had boosted screwball comedies by creating an audience looking for escapism, it was the impending war in Europe that changed the nature of comedy. Now it was the turn of the English.

In 1938, in order to boost morale among the British troops, the Entertainments National Service Association was formed, known to all as ENSA. Not only did they recruit entertainers to perform for the troops wherever they were stationed, but they also organized variety shows that were recorded and transmitted by the BBC, with music and comedy high on the programme. This proved to be a fertile ground for comedians to develop their acts and explore new avenues for humour, without having to worry too much about censorship. The benefits were seen when the war was over with a new genre of brilliant comedies made at the Ealing Studios in West London.

The Second World War created a need for people to learn to cope with misfortune by laughing at it and that was what inspired the black comedies from Ealing. The themes were usually serious and tended to be exactly what the Hays Code had sought to stamp out in America, but they were treated in a hilarious manner by a cast that consisted not so much of traditional comedians who could act a little, but very good actors with an extra talent for comedy.

Kind Hearts and Coronets (1949) was the story of a man who plans to murder a large number of his relatives in order to inherit the family title and wealth. *The Lavender Hill Mob* (1951) told the unlikely tale of a modest artist and an unambitious bank clerk who together plan and execute a massive gold bullion robbery. *The Ladykillers* (1955) featured a criminal gang whose members are split on whether or not to murder a sweet old lady to prevent her giving them away. All of those films starred Alec Guinness, who displayed true comic genius in playing eight different parts in *Kind Hearts and Coronets* and went on to become one of Britain's finest character actors.

Between 1947 and 1958, Ealing studios made 19 comedy films, of which around half were in the black comedy mould they had created, and which fitted the mood of the nation perfectly. Very funny, anarchic and confident, this was a new comedy for the new world order that was being built.

Meanwhile, back in America, the Hays Code was coming increasingly under strain as the movie industry devised ingenious ways to get around it, generally by following it to the letter but not in spirit. In 1952, the US Supreme Court ruled that the Hays Code was unconstitutional, as it offended every American's First Amendment right to free speech.

That decision put an end to federally sanctioned movie censorship, but local censor boards struggled on for more than a decade to assert their moral values. Some credit Billy Wilder's 1959 comedy *Some Like It Hot* with hastening its final demise. The plot, featuring Jack Lemmon and Tony Curtis dressing up as women to escape gangsters, blurred traditional gender boundaries so much that strict application of the Code was difficult if not impossible. Even when Jack Lemmon climbed into Marilyn Monroe's bunk on a train with both seen to have their feet off the floor, it was not clearly offending any of the Code's stipulations. Predictably, the film was condemned by the League for Decency and was banned in Kansas.

Yet over America as a whole, *Some Like It Hot* was a great success and earned six Academy Award nominations. Its only win, however, was for Best Costume Design, though it was not clear whether that referred to the dresses worn by Jack Lemmon and Tony Curtis. The popularity and general critical praise for the film showed that America had moved on from the era of censorship and strict control that Will H. Hays had imposed. The black comedies from Ealing and the sexual hilarity of *Some Like It Hot* paved the way for liberation in the cinema and ushered in a golden era of screen comedy.

Slapstick, screwball and black comedies continued, but were soon accompanied by several other genres. Action comedies, such as the *Pirates of the Caribbean* series or anything with Jackie Chan proved to be very popular, while parody comedies, such as Mel Brooks's *Blazing Saddles* and *Young Frankenstein* or Leslie Nielsen's *Naked Gun* and *Airplane!*, achieved great success by mercilessly spoofing more serious films. Even musicals were not immune, with Richard O'Brien's *Rocky Horror Picture Show* in 1975, followed by *The Blues Brothers* (1980) and *Little Shop of Horrors* (1986). In 1999, the movie *South Park: Bigger, Longer and Uncut* set new standards for rule-breaking by gaining an NC-17 (No Child 17 or under admitted) rating from the Motion Picture Association of America. For an animated, comedy musical to gain this highest rating of disapproval was a clear sign that comedy had at last broken all the rules.

11

RADIO AND TV

*"This is Bob 'Football' Hope telling you to always use
Pepsodent because it's better to set out for a nice run than
to run out for a nice set!"*
Bob Hope on *The Pepsodent Show*, 1938

Two television aerials met on a roof, fell in love and got married.
The ceremony wasn't great but the reception was fantastic ...

BBC Radio began its daily broadcasts in 1922; the BBC
Television Service began in 1936, but for each, it took more than
a decade before comedy became a regular feature. The BBC saw
as part of its duty a responsibility to uphold the moral standards
of the nation, so was very cautious about the contents of its
broadcasts. Comedy programmes were a particular problem as it
was in the nature of comedy to be spontaneous and spontaneity
was frowned upon as it could not be vetted in advance. In 1948,
the corporation even produced, for internal circulation among
producers and writers, a "Green Book" outlining its policies
toward what it called "light entertainment". The document
did, however, point out that "it cannot replace the need of each
producer to exercise continued vigilance in matters of taste". Its
rules and recommendations, however, even made some of the
Hays Code look liberal by comparison.

The aim of the BBC, the Green Book explained, "is for its
programmes to entertain without giving reasonable offence to
any part of its diversified audience. It must therefore keep its
programmes free from vulgarity, political bias, and matter in
questionable taste." Under the heading "Vulgarity", it stated

that: "Programmes must at all cost be kept free of crudities, coarseness and innuendo. Humour must be clean and untainted directly or by association with vulgarity and suggestiveness. Music hall, stage, and to a lesser degree, screen standards, are not suitable to broadcasting."

Warming to its task, the Green Book then announced an absolute ban on "jokes about Lavatories, Effeminacy in men, Immorality of any kind, Suggestive references to Honeymoon couples, Chambermaids, Fig leaves, Prostitution, Ladies' underwear, e.g. winter draws on, Animal habits, e.g. rabbits, Lodgers, Commercial travellers." Extreme care was advised in the case of jokes about pre-natal influences or marital infidelity. There followed a long set of pieces of advice about matters such as religion, politics and even music ("the jazzing by dance bands of classical tunes . . . is normally unacceptable"). It ended its 16 pages by pointing out that "Chinese laundry jokes may be offensive" and "jokes about harems are offensive in some parts of the world".

Radio comedy in America was quicker off the mark, with advertisers seizing the opportunity to promote their products by sponsoring comedy programmes which they knew would be popular. Bob Hope, for example, had already established himself as a vaudeville star with a large fan base by the time he was invited to present *The Pepsodent Show* on NBC.

For the BBC, the situation was also delayed by the fact that many of the best music hall comedians had followed Charlie Chaplin into the American movie business and the shortage grew worse when the Second World War began as even more joined ENSA to entertain the troops. When the war was over, everyone, including the BBC, relaxed and the 1950s brought some wonderfully imaginative, anarchic and truly funny performers to British radios with regular series such as *The Goon Show* and *Hancock's Half Hour*, both of which showed a spirit of liberality that the compilers of the Green Book must have abhorred. The Goons especially produced a style of surreal, zany comedy that was perfect for radio. The words, sounds and characters dreamed up by a cast led by Spike Milligan, Peter Sellers and Harry Secombe created bizarre images in listeners' minds that would have been far less effective if they could see what was happening.

Radio and television, however, brought a new problem for comedians raised on vaudeville or music halls. In those days, they had performed to only a few hundred people every night with the result that they could repeat the same act and tell the same jokes night after night, then take the same routine to another theatre and do it again. As radios and televisions spread, however, their best jokes could be heard by millions in one performance. Never before had performers needed a constant supply of new material, and the golden age of the comedy scriptwriter had begun.

During the music-hall era in Britain and the vaudeville period in the US, comedians generally wrote their own material, developed their act, and then stuck with it at various venues. The biggest, most successful and therefore most lucrative circuit for British performers was the Moss Empires company formed in 1898 by Sir Edward Moss and Sir Oswald Stoll. They built on the popularity of music hall by designing theatres to cope with the demand in almost every main city and seaside resort in Britain, creating a circuit of 33 music halls. With two performances in the evenings and occasional matinees, this kept the best comedians in constant employment with minimal modification to their material. Their contracts were also liable to include a non-broadcast clause, as the theatre management recognized the threat posed by radio and television: once a comedian's routine was transmitted on radio or television, there would be a drastic reduction in the number of people wanting to buy theatre tickets to hear or see it repeated.

A regular spot on the radio or television, of course, was both lucrative and wonderful for a comedian's reputation, though the need to generate new material was very demanding, which is where the scriptwriters came in. Even Morecambe and Wise, who became perhaps the most popular TV comic act ever, had spent around 15 years together touring the music halls with little change in their act before television changed everything and catapulted them to fame. When they appeared on ITV in the 1960s, their scripts were mostly written by Dick Hills and Sid Green, and when they moved to BBC, Eddie Braben took over their scriptwriting and created the characters that became the nation's favourites.

In the old music-hall days, the performer may have been just a comedian but now they all had to be true comic actors. Morecambe and Wise may have been *Two of a Kind*, as one of their early television series was called, but the alliance with Braben formed a real threesome, all of whom were essential for creating and delivering the final product. Similarly, Ray Galton and Alan Simpson were the scriptwriters behind both *Hancock's Half Hour* (1954–61) and *Steptoe and Son* (1962–74), which were two of the most successful comedy series of the time. Other great comedy scriptwriters active in the UK during this period include Johnny Speight, who wrote sketches for Arthur Haynes, Arthur Askey and Frankie Howerd and then went on to create *Till Death Us Do Part*; and David Nobbs, who wrote for Frankie Howerd, Ken Dodd, Dick Emery and Tommy Cooper and went on to become the highly esteemed comic author of novels such as *The Fall and Rise of Reginald Perrin*, which also became a TV series.

Across the Atlantic, a different manner of creating comedy television emerged, with more of the writers becoming great performers themselves and more of the comedians having established teams rather than just one or two scriptwriters working for them. Sid Caesar, who was the funniest and most successful US comic in the 1950s, appearing on *Your Show of Shows* (1950–4) and hosting *Caesar's Hour* (1954–7). The writers working for him on those were the finest comics of their generation, including Mel Brooks, Neil Simon, Danny Simon, Larry Gelbart and Woody Allen, all of whom went on to illustrious careers of their own.

The 1950s was the decade in which comedy saw its greatest changes. The decade began with only around 200,000 people in Britain having television licences, but by 1960 there were over ten million. Music halls had been in decline since the time of the First World War and with the increase of excellent variety shows on both radio and television, their demise was certain. By the early 1960s, the theatres that hosted them had all moved on to other types of entertainment.

Many of the old-style comedians could not meet the demands of the new media so failed to make the transition from music hall and were left to fade away. Those that discovered the knack of radio and television founded a golden age of comedy, but there was even better to come.

If you look up the word "sitcom" in the *OED*, you will discover that it entered the English language in 1956, but its origins lay in Galton and Simpson's radio scripts for *Hancock's Half Hour* and Eddie Braben's scripts that moulded Morecambe and Wise for television. In both cases, the key to their success was to create consistent roles that the leading characters could fill every week, though the stories and jokes would change. The role that was moulded for Hancock was that of a misanthropic, down-at-heel snob, living in poverty with Bill Kerr as his Australian lodger and Sid James as his totally untrustworthy friend and confidant whose schemes always led to trouble. Some say that Hancock's role was just an extreme exaggeration of his own personality. Something similar was done with Morecambe and Wise, but in their case it was the genuine friendship between the two men that was brought into their act and exaggerated to the point that they lived together and shared a bed in their shows – which they only agreed to when it was pointed out to them that Laurel and Hardy had shared a bed in their films too. Hancock's programmes were basically one-act plays with a different plot every week involving the same characters. Morecambe and Wise, on the other hand, performed comedy sketches, but the effect was greatly enhanced by bringing in the strong relationship between them. In both cases, a feeling of warmth was created in the audience by emphasizing a familiar thread that always ran through the story and held it together.

With hindsight, we may say that the first television sitcom of all, long before the word "sitcom" was coined, was *Pinwright's Progress*, transmitted live by the BBC in 1946–7. It was about a likeable shop owner with a loyal but incompetent staff, which included a deaf messenger boy in his eighties, and each of its ten episodes centred on problems created by a particular hated rival. Sadly this was in the days before recordings were possible, so accounts of it are vague, but all the features a sitcom needs were clearly there.

In 1951, American television audiences started watching *I Love Lucy*, which quickly became the most popular show in the US. Centred on the family of Lucille Ball and Desi Arnaz, who were a real-life married couple as well as playing those roles on-screen, it introduced factors that were to become characteristic of the sitcom genre.

Until then, most TV programmes were transmitted live and were necessarily unedited. One major difference of *I Love Lucy* was that it was filmed by three cameras and the images edited together to show everything from the most appropriate angle. This created inconsistency in the recordings of laughter from the live audience which was solved by dubbing a laughter track onto the sound of the actors.

The idea of "canned laughter" as it came to be known originated in 1949 when a Mexican sound engineer named Charley Douglass created the "laff box", a device with a large number of buttons that could be pressed to activate records he had made of different types of laughter, from giggle to guffaw, polite to raucous, made by young and old, male and female audiences. Choosing which buttons to press in order to simulate the right sort of laughter became an art in itself. It was first used on *The Hank McCune Show* in 1949, which was performed without a studio audience. Not only did it fill the awkward silence after jokes but the social aspect of laughter was quickly found to make programmes seem funnier: people laughed because they heard others laughing.

Thanks to the movie-like filming and editing, its natural family setting and the laff box, *I Love Lucy* became the most watched programme on US television and quickly led to dozens more sitcoms trying to portray sympathetic characters with whom the audience could identify. Perhaps best of all was the fact that sitcoms were cheap: the sets were the same every week and so were the characters, which demanded less rehearsal time and enabled the writers of each episode to move directly into the plot without introducing everyone.

A great deal has been written about the art of writing sitcoms and many different and often contradictory pieces of advice have been offered on the perfect formula. What follows is a distillation of what seem to me to be the essential features behind all of these:

The Characters: These are designed to portray certain easily recognized personality traits that are exaggerated usually to an extreme extent. In many cases these will be traits the viewer recognizes in themself, but exaggerated to a degree that they become laughable. The audience are thus laughing at extreme versions of themselves.

Plot: According to Aristotle, a whole is that which has a beginning, middle and end. He was writing about tragedy at the time but what he said is just as important in an episode of a sitcom. However, in a sitcom, the beginning has to be established as quickly as possible, the middle must create enough comic mayhem to keep the story going and the end must resolve it; or, as several writers have modified Aristotle's formula: it must have a beginning, a muddle and an end.

Location: A stable location for all or most episodes both cuts costs and offers instant familiarity to the viewers. Whether this is a taxi office (*Taxi*), a hotel (*Fawlty Towers*), a bar (*Cheers*) or a prison (*Porridge*), a stable and recognizable location always helps get each episode off to a quick start.

Jokes: Good sitcoms have no jokes: instead they have witty and succinct comments that are perfectly in line with the personalities they portray. This is why the characters must be defined so clearly: the secret is to create the plot and then let the characters write the script. That realization was what finally explained to me why some of the best American sitcoms have large teams of scriptwriters. How can a team of people write anything together without disintegrating into an almighty squabble? The answer is that once the characters and the story-line are established, much of the task of writing the perfect script consists of coming up with the perfect, in-character responses to other characters' questions or comments. A team of competing scriptwriters can enjoy all having the same goal while vying with each other to produce funnier lines.

Defining the characters well is the key to any good sitcom. In his book *The Eight Characters of Comedy: A Guide to Sitcom Acting & Writing*, the American author and acting coach Scott Sedita identifies eight roles: 1. The Logical Smart One; 2. The Lovable Loser; 3. The Neurotic; 4. The Dumb One; 5. The Bitch/Bastard; 6. The Womanizer; 7. The Materialistic One; 8. In Their Own Universe. Most often, however, a character may fill more than one of those roles, which is fortunate as eight characters is far too many to fit comfortably on one sofa, which most sitcoms find a useful way of establishing the togetherness of the cast. Of course, all the characters in *Third Rock from the Sun* are in their own universe, being aliens from another galaxy, and they can also be alternately Logical Smart Ones, when they show their superior knowledge to that of mere earthlings, and Dumb Ones when they are trapped by their lack of understanding of human traits. But the character of Sally is definitely a female alien equivalent of The Womanizer.

Quite apart from eight being a high number of characters, I would add a ninth: the normal person. The more the main characters are beyond belief, the more a sitcom needs a normal person to be affected by what is going on and to be easy for the audience to identify with. This is especially valuable when the humour relies on a misunderstanding or differing interpretations of the same thing. In such cases it can be very useful to have a rational person around who understands exactly what is happening. Connie Booth's character Polly in *Fawlty Towers* is a perfect example of this: she is both the least responsible for the comedy but the best to help the audience appreciate it.

All agree that the disputes in a sitcom stem from well-defined personality differences between the main characters, but despite the above eight or nine character types, the most popular number of principal roles in a sitcom is four, which appropriately is the number than can be accommodated, with a little squeeze perhaps, on a sofa. Several writers have insisted that four is the right number of characters but there are different versions of who these roles should represent. One popular theory is that they should be a hero, an anti-hero, a love interest and a buddy, while another theory is that they should adopt personalities taken from the commedia dell'arte in late Renaissance Italy: patriarch, matriarch, craftsman and clown.

Several successful sitcoms have had four main characters, but it is easier accommodating them all together on a sofa than forcing them into the above foursome sets. You may like to try to do so with the following:

- *I Love Lucy*: Lucy, Ricky, Fred, Ethel
- *Third Rock From the Sun*: Dick, Sally, Harry, Tommy
- *Cheers*: Sam, Coach, Norm, Cliff – until Diane arrived as a love interest and Frasier brought the number up to six
- *The Young Ones*: Rick, Vyv, Neil, Mike – all of whom could be seen as clowns
- *Fawlty Towers*: Basil, Sybil, Polly, Manuel, which may be the best fit to the commedia dell'arte model
- *Seinfeld*: Jerry, Elaine, George, Cosmo

Even *South Park* had Cartman, Kyle, Stan and Kenny, who were totally lacking a love element, while *Big Bang Theory* had

Sheldon, Leonard, Howard and Raj, and only included a love interest when they were joined by Penny and Bernadette.

For half a century after *I Love Lucy* first hit TV screens, sitcoms featured high in the list of most-watched programmes. From 1952–3 to 1954–5, *I Love Lucy* itself topped the list of most watched programmes, again reaching the top of the list in 1956–7. *Beverly Hillbillies* was top in 1962–3 and 1963–4, while *All in the Family* was the most popular programme for five years in a row from 1971–2 until 1975–6. After that, *Happy Days, Laverne & Shirley, Roseanne, Cheers, Seinfeld* and *Friends* all took their turns at the top, while in the UK, *Love Thy Neighbour* in 1974, *To the Manor Born* in 1979, and *Only Fools and Horses in* 1996 all became the most-watched programmes of the year.

Sitcoms have somewhat faded in popularity since this glorious era for a number of reasons: perhaps it was because the audience tired of laugh tracks, which they increasingly saw as manipulative by telling them when to laugh; perhaps it was partly that other programmes slowly took up the challenge posed by sitcoms and became much better; but most of all, the growing number of TV channels brought by satellite and cable technology brought increasing competition, making it ever more difficult to attract large audiences. In fact, one of the greatest reasons for new sitcoms achieving smaller shares of the audience has been the competition from repeats of other older sitcoms.

Interestingly, one area in which sitcoms have increased in popularity and versatility has been animation. It started in 1960 with *The Flintstones*, which was a classic four-main-character sitcom set in the Stone Age and following the adventures of Fred and Wilma Flintstone and Barney and Betty Rubble. It ran for six years and became the first animated series to be screened at a prime time. Its total of 166 episodes was almost as many as the 188 of *I Love Lucy*.

Other, later series achieved more episodes, with *Cheers* recording 275 and *Big Bang Theory* 279, but these figures were overtaken by *South Park* (318) and *Family Guy* (389) and have been totally dwarfed by the 728 episodes (by mid-2022) of *The*

Simpsons. Both Bart Simpson and Eric Cartman of *South Park* have stayed at the age of ten for decades, which is one great advantage of animation: the actors never age, so their sitcoms can go on for ever.

We shall have much more to say about what cartoons and animation bring to humour in the next chapter, so let's stop there.

12
CARTOONS

"If cartoons were meant for adults, they'd put them on in prime time."

Lisa in *The Simpsons*

A man walked into a doctor's surgery and told the doctor that he feared he was turning into a cartoon rabbit. After hearing the man's symptoms, the doctor said: "You have a bad case of updoc."

"What's updoc?" the patient asked and the doctor said: "This is more serious than I thought."

The word "cartoon" has a curious history. When it first appeared in the late 17th century, it referred to a drawing or painting on stout card. That is the sense still used when we refer to the Leonardo da Vinci cartoon, for example, which was drawn almost 200 years before the word was coined in English. *Cartone* in Italian just meant a large sheet of paper such as an artist might use for a preliminary sketch for a painting.

The English meaning changed in 1843 when the British humorous magazine *Punch* announced: "*Punch* has the benevolence to announce, that in an early number of his ensuing Volume he will astonish the Parliamentary Committee by the publication of several exquisite designs, to be called Punch's Cartoons!"

The very first such cartoon, drawn by John Leech and appropriately captioned "Cartoon, No.1", was titled *Substance and Shadow*. It was a drawing of crippled children and waifs looking at paintings of wealthy and privileged individuals that was intended to accompany a satirical editorial criticizing a government announcement that it would sponsor an exhibition of such paintings. The editorial ran as follows:

> There are many silly, dissatisfied people in this country, who are continually urging upon Ministers the propriety of considering the wants of the pauper population, under the impression that it is as laudable to feed men as to shelter horses.
>
> To meet the views of such unreasonable people, the Government would have to put its hand into the money-box. We would ask how the Chancellor of the Exchequer can be required to commit such an act of folly, knowing, as we do, that the balance of the budget was triflingly against him, and that he has such righteous and paramount claims upon him as the Duke of Cumberland's income, the Duchess of Mecklenburg Strelitz's pin-money, and the builder's little account for the Royal Stables.
>
> We conceive that the Ministers have adopted the very best means to silence this unwarrantable outcry. They have considerably determined that as they cannot afford to give hungry nakedness the substance which it covets, at least it shall have the shadow.
>
> The poor ask for bread, and the philanthropy of the State accords – an exhibition.

The use of the word "cartoon" for Leech's brilliant drawings was part of the satire: it was a word previously used to describe works of art that were available only to rich people and establishment figures whom *Punch* was satirizing. The term naturally spread to cover all drawings in *Punch*, particularly those by Leech who contributed some 3,000 cartoons to the magazine as its principal artist.

Leech's other great achievement in 1843 was to be chosen by Charles Dickens to illustrate his story *A Christmas Carol*. Leech's striking picture of the Ghost of Christmas Past has been held by many to have been as important as Dickens' writing in ensuring the success of the book.

Thanks to Leech and *Punch,* cartoons became an important part of British national humour and their role grew significantly as the Second World War loomed. In 1939, the *Daily Express* introduced a major innovation in the form of something that soon came to be known as a "pocket cartoon". Leech's cartoons for *Punch* had started as full-page pictures, but the new pocket cartoons (named incidentally in mockery of the German pocket battleships) were only one newspaper column in width so took up little room on the page and could be placed more or less anywhere. The *Express* recruited Osbert Lancaster to draw them and he continued doing so for 42 years until his retirement in 1981.

Lancaster's style was popular from the start. His cartoons were soon moved to the front page and the novel aspect was that they were, above everything else, funny. Before these, cartoons had been vehicles of satire, designed primarily to heap scorn on certain people or government policies. Lancaster's themes often included something similar, but that was not their main aim. He did not want to make people angry, he wanted to make them laugh, which he did brilliantly.

With the international situation so tense, people needed something that enabled them to see the funny side of serious matters, to deflate pomposity and to support the increasing assertiveness of the middle classes – and the pocket cartoon did all those things. Other newspapers copied the idea and since then, pocket cartoons have been a common feature of many serious newspaper front pages.

While all this was going on, however, another major enlargement in the meaning of "cartoon" had been steadily growing since 1916. This was the use of the word to describe animations, though such clever blends of drawing and technology had first appeared some years previously. The very first animated cartoon was created by the French caricaturist

Émile Cohl in 1908 and was called *Fantasmagorie*. It was made from 700 drawings on glass plates, depicting a stick man encountering various objects that transformed into other objects. One sequence showed a wine bottle turning into a flower that then became an elephant.

Cohl's technique for creating it involved making each drawing by placing a new glass plate on top of the previous one, then making another drawing showing a small change. Finally, he photographed all the drawings and used the negatives of the photographs to make a film, thus reversing the black-and-white images to make his ink drawings look like white chalk on a blackboard.

Fantasmagorie inspired the start of the animated cartoon industry, leading to the appearance of Gertie the Dinosaur in 1914, who quickly became extinct and was replaced by Felix the Cat in 1919, and, in 1928, Mickey Mouse made his first appearance in *Steamboat Willie*. After that, a rush of humorous cartoon characters made their mark, led by the spinach-eating Popeye in 1929, the slinky Betty Boop in 1930 and Donald Duck in 1934. One remarkable effect of this was that in the US, the name "Donald" was given to 30,408 newborn boys and 110 girls in the year 1934, which is still the highest number ever. After the fall of Donald Trump, incidentally, the number of newborn Donalds fell to an all-time low of 444 in 2020, compared to 507 in 2019 and 602 in 2017. Never since the name first appeared in the 1880s has it been less popular.

In 1937, in Crystal City, Texas, which proclaims itself the Spinach Capital of the World, Popeye became the first cartoon character to have a statue erected in his honour. This feat was outdone in 1997, however, when Bugs Bunny became the first cartoon character to appear on a US postage stamp. Bugs, incidentally, whose official debut was in 1940, was listed in ninth place in 2011 by Guinness World Records in a list of characters depicted in the most films. With 229 appearances, he appeared on the list between Sherlock Holmes and Dracula. Other lists, however, have placed Mickey Mouse even higher.

There have been many attempts to explain what makes animated cartoon films so funny and therefore so popular, but the main reason must be that cartoons enable some things to be depicted with an ease that even modern techniques of CGI (Computer Generated Imagery) cannot achieve so easily or effectively with human actors. Most impressive of all, however, is the way in which cartoon characters can break the laws of physics.

In the same way that simply breaking the law is not enough of a plot for a crime film, the real achievement of cartoon animation is not just law-breaking, but the manner in which it has created its own laws and sticks to them. In 1980, the US writer and humourist Mark O'Donnell updated Newton to list the Laws of Cartoon Motion for *Esquire* magazine and later expanded in his book *Elementary Education*. Here are his ten laws:

1. Any body suspended in space will remain in space until made aware of its situation.
2. Any body in motion will tend to remain in motion until solid matter intervenes.
3. Any body passing through solid matter will leave a perforation conforming to its perimeter.
4. The time required for an object to fall twenty stories is greater than or equal to the time it takes for whoever knocked it off the ledge to spiral down twenty flights to attempt to capture it unbroken.
5. All principles of gravity are negated by fear.
6. As speed increases, objects can be in several places at once.
7. Certain bodies can pass through solid walls painted to resemble tunnel entrances; others cannot.
8. Any violent rearrangement of feline matter is impermanent.
9. For every vengeance there is an equal and opposite revengeance.
10. Everything falls faster than an anvil.

Most of these can be expanded to give more precise laws. For example, the first law often covers the case of a character running off the edge of a cliff, when his motion continues on a straight path until he realizes there is nothing below his feet, at which point he will come screeching to an abrupt halt and then plummet vertically downwards. On hitting the ground, an evil character will shatter into a million pieces but a good one will either be rescued by something travelling across the precise point of impact at the right moment or he will just continue running as though nothing happened. This law is occasionally simplified to say that gravity only begins to work when you look down.

Other cartoon laws have been added to the above. Here are some of the best:

11. A sharp object, especially when applied to the buttocks, will propel a character vertically upwards.
12. Explosions never kill but can only turn characters black and smoky.
13. Any bag or case will be big enough to contain any objects stuffed or dropped into it, however large they may be.
14. Movements of characters are always accompanied by funny sound effects.
15. Any body in motion continues in motion until it splats into a solid surface, when it will either shatter or Law 7, above, will be invoked.
16. All of the above will only occur if it is funny to do so.

Interestingly, such laws of cartoon physics gave everyone two chances to take a bite of the cheerfulness: the first was caused by the surprise created by an incident at variance with normal expectations, but the second lies in the reassuring familiarity of the cartoon world sticking to its own laws.

While the world of animated cartoons was evolving in this manner, another related genre of cartoon humour was developing in the same era but as far as humour was concerned hit more of an evolutionary dead end.

The phrase "comic strip"' only entered the English language around 1913, though the idea of telling funny stories through a number of cartoons had been popular in France, Belgium and Switzerland since the 1820s, and *Mutt and Jeff,* the first amusing daily newspaper comic strip, began in the *San Francisco Chronicle* in 1907.

Of course, telling stories in pictures was much older. The Japanese had been producing what they called *manga* for centuries, while you could say that the Bayeux Tapestry, portraying the story of the Battle of Hastings in 1066, was a very early French version, but such examples were not intended to provoke humour.

Bud Fisher's *Mutt and Jeff,* however, took its cue from the comic success of cartoons in Britain and the US; and similar strip cartoons led to the development of comic books, usually with superhero themes, in the US and comics such as *The Dandy* (1937) and *The Beano* (1938), geared to appeal specifically to children in the UK.

As animated films became more sophisticated and funnier, however, comic books in the US went increasingly in the direction of superheroes and action stories, while the circulation of *The Beano,* which had been over a million copies for each issue in the 1950, had dropped to around 34,000 by 2017. *The Dandy,* which had reached two million copies a week in the 1950s, had slumped to 8,000 a week when its printed edition came to an end in 2012.

With too many children glued to their televisions and other screens, the era of printed comics had faded and given way to a new and glorious era of TV animations, which began in 1960 with *The Flintstones* but went on to reach new comic heights and break all taboos with the launch of *The Simpsons* in 1989, *South Park* in 1997 and *Family Guy* in 1999, all of which challenged the increasing encroachment of humourless political correctness.

The Flintstones took a vital step in the emancipation of animated cartoons. Created by Joseph Barbera and William Hanna, who had also given *Tom and Jerry* to the world, it was the first prime-time animated TV series and the first to be written for both children and adults to enjoy. The idea behind it was to create a satire on the American way of life by setting the story in the Stone Age, with Fred Flintstone, his wife Wilma and their neighbours Barney and Betty Rubble displaying all the foibles of modernity while having to cope with the primitive technology of their times.

Some of the early reviews, however, missed the point. The day after its first programme, *Variety* magazine reviewed it beneath a huge front-page headline saying: "Flintstones a Pen and Ink Disaster". The public, however, disagreed and it became a huge hit, with its initial series running for six years. Quite apart from the brilliant anachronism of moving modern problems a long way back in time, the series was able to use its animated cartoon format to portray some aspects of human behaviour that they could not have done had they used human actors: showing Fred and Wilma sharing a bed, for example, was still one aspect of normality that would have attracted severe censure if actors had done it.

When Matt Groening created *The Simpsons* in 1989, he further exploited the possibilities of using cartoons to portray behaviour that was either impossible or unacceptable when humans were involved. Just as the violence in *Tom and Jerry* or *Bugs Bunny* was seen by both adults and children as funny, the behavioural traits of Homer and Bart Simpson became acceptable and humorous because they were so exaggerated. As with *The Flintstones*, however, not everyone saw the joke.

One US newspaper in 1990 ran a story about a school principal who banned Bart Simpson T-shirts that said "under-achiever and proud of it", quoting the teacher as saying that, "It teaches the wrong thing to students." And even the President expressed strong doubts about *The Simpsons*. In 1992, in a speech in Wisconsin, George Bush said this: "It's time, high time, that we change America, time to turn our attention to pressing challenges like . . . how to make American families more like the Waltons and a little bit less like the Simpsons."

Yet just like *Variety* magazine and the school principal quoted above, the President got it wrong. The Simpsons were not such a bad influence and, more important, they were much funnier than the Waltons. Matt Groening had a good reply to Bush's assessment of the programme: "Hey, the Simpsons are just like the Waltons. Both families are praying for the end of the Depression."

In an article in May 1990, *Entertainment Weekly* was spot on in its assessment: "Groening has invested Bart – and all the other Simpsons for that matter – with a sensitive, vulnerable side that most sitcoms with human beings lack. In the standard sitcom, kids are obnoxious, moms are long-suffering, and dads are dopes. They're the cartoons; the Simpsons are for real." Bart Simpson (whose first name, probably intentionally, is an anagram of 'Brat'), they described as "rude because he doesn't fit in with the world, which has already hurt his feelings a few times too many". They summed up their assessment by saying that: "The Simpsons are the American family at its most complicated, drawn as simple cartoons." And Homer, however often he seems to be trying to strangle Bart, always lets his feelings and obligations toward his family eventually overrule his selfishness, however reluctant he may be to do so. The difficult battle between these two objectives lies at the heart of the humour and the appeal of the programme.

At the end of 1999, *Time* magazine published a list of the "100 Most Influential People of the 20th Century" and perhaps the biggest surprise on the list was its inclusion of Bart Simpson. Bruce Handy, a senior writer at Time, said that what Bart in particular and *The Simpsons* in general had done was to "merge social satire with popular animation in a way that hasn't really been done before".

He argued that you can't discuss contemporary art without taking pop culture into account and that was almost what defined the 20th century. He also described animation as "arguably the purelt form of cinema" and expressed his own belief that *The Simpsons* was first rate and of lasting quality. And to emphasize what he was saying, he expressed his confidence that people will still be viewing *The Simpsons* long into the future and even a hundred years from now it will give people a perfect sense of what the 1990s were like. "It will still be being viewed and enjoyed when a lot of contemporary, serious literature is forgotten."

Joseph Barbera had proved with *The Flintstones* that the comic appeal of animation could be extended beyond a child audience. Comic dinosaurs may have been enough to attract children but the essential anachronism of the show was what grown-ups loved. To appreciate anachronism properly requires a sense of history, and placing modern morals in a prehistoric setting was a stroke of animated genius.

Once the adult appeal of animation had been established, Matt Groenig took it a stage further with *The Simpsons*, which was essentially a parody of sitcoms featuring deliciously vulgar characters with hearts of gold. The success of *The Simpsons* led almost inevitably to funnier and still more politically incorrect animated comedies in which at least some of the characters had hearts of purest stone, with Trey Parker and Matt Stone's *South Park* and Seth MacFarlane's *Family Guy* leading the way. Before coming to these, however, we must praise another American TV series which in many ways paved the comedic way for these programmes, despite not using animation but real actors. But that was, perhaps, the real problem that faced *Soap*, which was screened between 1977 and 1981 and delighted or infuriated its late-night audience in about equal measures.

Conceived and written by Susan Harris, *Soap* was a superb parody of all other television soap operas. In common with all of them, each episode of *Soap* featured another ludicrously dramatic turn of events for the families it followed, ending with a cliff-hanger to tempt viewers to tune in again for the next episode to see what happened. In contrast to the other soaps, however, these cliff-hanging problems involved homosexuality, alien abduction, kidnapping, murder, racism, the mentally ill, incest, impotence, extramarital affairs, demonic possession, cults and everything else that had been banned or at least regarded with intense suspicion since the days of the Hays Code.

Various Churches put aside their differences and united in condemnation of the programme and strongly advised their followers not to watch it. Perhaps most remarkable of all, the Los Angeles Archdiocese of the Roman Catholic Church urged American families to boycott it and the Board of Rabbis of Southern California said that the show "reached a new low". Rarely had the Roman Catholic Church and Judaism reached such an accord. And as if to show this was not just a religious objection to the moral tone of the programme, the International Union of Gay Athletes also voiced strong disapproval of the way they suspected it would portray homosexuality. In hindsight, this stand was particularly misconceived as Billy Crystal's sensitive portrayal of Jodie Dallas was outstandingly successful in positively transforming the audience's opinions of gay people.

Most objections to *Soap* were based on hearsay and were made before the series began to be screened. When the first episode was shown on 3 September 1977, a poll at a university in Virginia reported that 74 per cent of viewers found it inoffensive, and, perhaps even more significantly, half of the 26 per cent who were offended said they would watch the second episode too – because above all, *Soap* was very, very funny and went on to win four Emmy awards.

Nevertheless, organized protests continued and after 93 episodes and four series, a planned fifth series was abruptly cancelled, mainly because of a worsening relationship between its TV network and their advertisers, who had been deluged with letters from offended viewers urging them not to support the programme with their advertisements.

Perhaps *Soap* was simply ahead of its time. Despite the fact that the humourless moralists were very much in the minority, they were a very vocal and influential minority and broadcasters worldwide took great care not to offend them. When Frank Muir was Assistant Head of BBC Light Entertainment and served as the corporation's consultant on comedy in the early 1960s, he received a memo reminding writers and comedians of a short list of taboos they should observe. In order of importance, they were: blasphemy, royalty, bodily infirmity, the colour question and homosexuality.

Typically, Frank Muir and his scriptwriting partner Denis Norden promptly coined a sentence to remind themselves what the forbidden topics were and their ranking order of severity (sensitive readers should insert asterisks where they think appropriate): "'Jesus Christ!' said the Queen. 'I do believe that one-eyed nigger's a poof.'" That sentence explains one of the features that made *Soap* so funny and successful before it was cancelled: just being disrespectful and disparaging to one minority, whether it is the Queen, the gay community, religion or something else, may be considered offensive, but making fun of all of them is making fun of prejudice itself, which is far more forgivable. Except when it isn't, of course, and leads to the cancellation of a series.

Yet Bart Simpson and *South Park*'s Eric Cartman adopt a similar scatter-gun approach to prejudice and intolerance, liable to be directed against any minority they happen to come across, so why have they thrived when, only a decade earlier, *Soap* had fallen victim to the politically correct brigade? One reason, no doubt, is due to a gradual change in society: we have become progressively more tolerant of the depiction of intolerance. Characters such as Alf Garnett in *Till Death Us Do Part* or Victor Meldrew in *One Foot in the Grave* became acceptable comic figures because the audience, for the most part, were laughing at them, not with them. As with all successful sitcoms, they were exaggerated versions of typical people and it was their prejudices we were laughing at, not the classes of people against whom they were prejudiced.

More important, however, was the fact that *The Simpsons*, *South Park* and *Family Guy* were animations, which enabled their creators to get away with far more. *Tom and Jerry* was considered suitable entertainment for children despite its level of violence precisely because the characters were an animated cat and a mouse and could not possibly be seen as role models. Bart and Cartman may have originally been seen by some as bad influences, but it was soon realized that the exaggerated cartoon nature of their characters acted as a protective shield. And by the time *Family Guy* came along with a talking dog and a highly sophisticated murderous baby in its cast, it had become clear that cartoons could get away with not just stretching the boundaries of what is permissible in comedy but effectively eliminating them entirely.

When the movie *South Park: Bigger, Longer and Uncut* was released in 1999, its creators Trey Parker and Matt Stone were amused and delighted for it to be classified as NC-17 by the ratings board, denying admittance to anyone under 17. After a few months this was changed to R (under-17s must be accompanied by a parent or adult guardian) but it had previously been unheard of for an animated comedy musical to receive such a rating.

After suffering a century of censorship, the new comic weapons of Bart Simpson, Eric Cartman, and Peter and Stewie Griffin and their dog Brian have demolished the old comic boundaries and made the world a funnier place. It is worth mentioning, however, that *Family Guy* was taken off the air after only two seasons, before being brought back when its DVD sales did so well that the Fox network realized that the viewers loved it.

So let's end with five quotations from each of these trend-setting animated shows for childish grown-ups and grown-up children that might well have been censored before they came along.

The Simpsons (all from Homer):

1. Oh, God gets your prayers, but he just clicks delete without reading them, like email updates from LinkedIn.
2. Marriage is like a coffin and each kid is another nail.
3. Facts are meaningless. You can use facts to prove anything that's even remotely true!

4. Marge, don't discourage the boy. Weaselling out of things is important to learn. It's what separates us from the animals, except the weasel.
5. But Marge, what if we picked the wrong religion? Each week we'd just make God madder and madder.

South Park:

1. Without evil there could be no good, so it must be good to be evil sometimes. (Cartman)
2. I'm sorry Wendy, but I just don't trust anything that bleeds for five days and doesn't die! (Mr. Garrison)
3. The only way to fight hate is with even more hate! (Cartman)
4. Everything's legal in Mexico, it's the American way. (Uncle Jimbo)
5. That's wrong, Cartman. But don't worry. There are no stupid answers, just stupid people. (Mr Garrison)

Family Guy:

1. Love is like a fart: if you have to force it, it's probably crap. (Peter Griffin)
2. Men aren't fat. Only fat women are fat. (Peter Griffin)
3. I guess we've learned that no matter who you are or where you come from, life is a terrible thing. (Peter Griffin)
4. If gays wanna get married and be miserable like the rest of us, I say we should let 'em. (Peter Griffin)
5. I love God. He's so deliciously evil. (Stewie Griffin)

13
COMIC NOVELS

"The stupidity of people comes from having an answer for everything. The wisdom of the novel comes from having a question for everything."

Milan Kundera, *The Book of Laughter and Forgetting*

A man went into a library and loudly asked the librarian for a portion of fish and chips. "This is a library, sir," she replied. "Oh, I'm sorry," he whispered. "Could I have a portion of fish and chips?"

Yesterday a book fell on my head, I have only my shelf to blame.

The art of writing humour is very different from telling jokes or acting in a comedy, just as the role of a playwright is different from that of an actor. Quite apart from the distinction between creating material and performing it, however, the task of writing a comic novel is also very different from writing other types of novel and has long been regarded with a degree of suspicion. Comic novelists do not win Nobel Literature prizes and the only times comic novels have won the Booker Prize were in 1986 and 2010 for works by Kingsley Amis and Howard Jacobsen respectively.

Announcing the Man-Booker winner in 2010, the chairman of the judges, former Poet Laureate Andrew Motion, said: "*The Finkler Question* should not be seen as something that was 'relentlessly middle-brow, or easy-peasy' because it was comic. It is much cleverer and more complicated and about much more difficult things than it immediately lets you know. Several people have used the word 'wise', and that's a good word."

The implication was that in general comic novels are a lower art form than other novels, aiming for easy popularity rather than anything profound. The authors of most of the earliest comic novels might be accused of sharing that viewpoint, for however funny the humorous parts of their books were, the works seemed always to contain a serious message as well. For a work to be respected as literature, comedy was not enough for even the greatest writers, as the following gallop through comic novel history testifies.

Miguel de Cervantes' *Don Quixote* has been described by many as the world's first comic novel and was generally seen as a comedy when its first part came out in 1605, yet later generations took a different view. In the 18th century, the adventures it depicts of a deluded Spanish gentleman in search of chivalry were thought of as being more of a tragedy and in the 19th century the work was primarily considered as a social commentary.

Equally, Tobias Smollett's first novel, *The Adventures of Roderick Random*, first published in 1748, was deliciously funny in its descriptions of surgery and the Royal Navy, but his satire was based on his own experiences as a naval-surgeon's mate. Whether his own experiences included being asked, during an examination at Surgeons' Hall, how he would behave "if, during an engagement at sea, a man should be brought to you with his head shot off", I do not know, but it provided a memorable comic moment in the book.

The picaresque style of *Roderick Random*, flitting from place to place as it followed the adventures of a slightly disreputable hero, established a fashion for comic novels in the 18th century, with Laurence Sterne and Henry Fielding following that pattern in *The Life and Opinions of Tristram Shandy* and *Tom Jones* respectively. While both books were basically joyous and occasionally salacious romps, however, both authors took every opportunity to bring their own philosophical views to the reader's attention and to provide a social commentary on their times.

For Sterne and Fielding, humour and social commentary were more or less equally important in their writings, but the balance shifted away from humour in fiction in the 19th century, even though the greatest social commentator of the age was also one of the best writers of humorous prose. For Charles Dickens knew better than any other writer how to lighten a serious message by injecting a touch of levity, as, for example, when he describes Mr Grimwig, just before the latter meets Oliver Twist in the novel of that name. He begins with a detailed description of his clothes, then tells us that: "the variety of shapes into which his countenance was twisted, defy description", and of course, he goes on immediately to describe it: "He had a manner of screwing his head on one side when he spoke; and of looking out of the corners of his eyes at the same time, which irresistibly reminded the beholder of a parrot."

Having set the scene, Dickens tells us what then happened:

In this attitude, he fixed himself, the moment he made
his appearance, and, holding out a small piece of
orange-peel at arm's length, exclaimed, in a growling,
discontented voice, —
    "Look here! do you see this! Isn't it a most wonderful
and extraordinary thing that I can't call at a man's house
but I find a piece of this poor surgeon's friend on the
staircase? I've been lamed with orange peel once, and I
know orange peel will be my death, or I'll be content to
eat my own head, sir!"
    This was the handsome offer with which Mr. Grimwig
backed and confirmed nearly every assertion he made;
and it was the more singular in his case, because, even
admitting, for the sake of argument, the possibility
of scientific improvements being brought to that pass
which will enable a gentleman to eat his own head in
the event of his being so disposed, Mr. Grimwig's head
was such a particularly large one, that the most sanguine
man alive could hardly entertain a hope of being able

to get through it at a sitting – to put entirely out of the question, a very thick coating of powder.

"I'll eat my head, sir," repeated Mr. Grimwig, striking his stick upon the ground.

To give such a detailed description of a minor character is a mark of genius and pure Dickens. It also makes us aware of an important difference between spoken or visual humour, on radio, television or stage for example, and written humour in novels: the first is delivered at a pace chosen by the humourist, the second is read at a pace determined by the reader, and is sometimes so funny that we go back a sentence or paragraph to read it again. The very length of the sentence explaining Mr Grimwig's "handsome offer" demands an immediate re-reading, for example, which adds to the reader's pleasure. The nature of comic timing is thus very different in novels.

Despite the genius of Dickens at humorous writing, however, we still had to wait for some time until someone came up with the idea of writing a novel that was solely intended to make us laugh. Surprisingly, in view of the tradition established in Britain by Smollett, Sterne and Fielding, that idea came from America. But perhaps it was not so surprising, for America, with its Revolution and Civil War, was eager to establish its own culture and strike out against the orthodoxy of European standards. And no one was better at creating his own standards than Samuel Clemens, or Mark Twain as he became better known.

Charles Dickens died in 1870 and Mark Twain's *The Adventures of Tom Sawyer* came out in 1876. He already had a good reputation as a humorous writer through newspaper columns he had written under such names as Thomas Jefferson Snodgrass, W. Epaminandos Adrastus Blab, Sergeant Fathom, and Josh, but in 1863 he had settled on "Mark Twain" as his pen-name, which was a nautical expression meaning "two fathoms deep". Under that name, he published in 1869 his first book, *The Innocents Abroad*, which was a collection of his newspaper writings about a trip around Europe. His short stories had already gained him the reputation of being a fine humourist, which was further enhanced by the wit shown in his travel writing. His gleefully exaggerated description of a town in Italy was typical: "It is well the alleys are not wider, because they hold as much smell now as a person can stand, and, of course, if they were wider they would hold more, and then the people would die."

With *Tom Sawyer*, however, Twain established a radical style that set new standards for comic novels and established his reputation worldwide. In both this book and the later *Adventures of Huckleberry Finn*, he abandoned the style of literary English that had previously been mandatory for respectable writers, instead letting the characters speak in colloquial vernacular language that might be ungrammatical but sounded convincingly authentic.

The American literary critic William Dean Howells was one of the first to recognize the genius of the man who called himself Mark Twain and wrote: "So far as I know, Mr. Clemens is the first writer to use in extended writing the fashion we all use in thinking, and to set down the thing that comes into his mind without fear or favor of the thing that went before or the thing that may be about to follow."

Twain sought out the man who had written such praise and when they met he thanked Howells in typically outrageous and funny style. In fact, his words were so offensive by today's standards that the publishers of this book refuse to print them. Nevertheless, it was the start of a lifelong friendship between Howells and Twain.

Later writers were just as enthusiastic in their praise for Mark Twain's literary accomplishments. The novelist Ralph Waldo Ellison in 1886 wrote that he "transformed elements of regional vernacular speech into a medium of uniquely American literary expression and thus taught us how to capture that which is essentially American in our folkways and manners. For indeed the vernacular process is a way of establishing and discovering our national identity." Ernest Hemingway, in *Green Hills of*

Africa (1935), goes further: "All modern American literature comes from one book by Mark Twain called *Huckleberry Finn* . . . it's the best book we've had. All American writing comes from that. There was nothing before. There has been nothing as good since."

Mark Twain may have been single-handedly responsible for breaking America out of the shackles of literary English comic writing, but it took two Englishmen to break England out of the same ingrained habit. George and Weedon Grossmith were brothers and their book, which was first published as a serial in *Punch* magazine, was *The Diary of a Nobody* (1892).

The tone is set in an introduction by the non-hero of the story, Mr Charles Pooter: "Why should I not publish my diary? I have often seen reminiscences of people I have never even heard of, and I fail to see – because I do not happen to be a 'Somebody' – why my diary should not be interesting. My only regret is that I did not commence it when I was a youth."

From this short introduction, the reader may immediately jump to the conclusion that the most interesting thing about Pooter is his remarkable degree of dullness, and the reader would not be wrong in that assessment. In fact, Pooter is so pompous and filled with such self-importance that he completely misses how dull he is as he tells us of his boring job, his tedious wife, his boring routine and the comings and goings of his equally dull neighbours Cummings and Gowing. The result is a masterpiece of self-indulgence which, after a slow start, has never been out of print since it first came out and which set a new tone for a glorious century of comic writing.

Remarkably, considering the critical and public acclaim of *Diary of a Nobody*, the Grossmith brothers never followed it up with anything similar. Weedon, the younger of the two, wrote a few plays and had a reasonably successful career as a comic actor, while George, who had earlier been a much-acclaimed stage performer in Gilbert and Sullivan operettas, gained considerable success as a solo performer of his own comic songs, even being acclaimed as the most popular such performer of the 1890s.

Their book, however, had finally let comic novelists in Britain off their leads to romp freely and serve up laughter without any moral or literary side salad. One of the first to take advantage of this new freedom and satisfy the growing public demand for well-written but undemanding humour was Pelham Grenville Wodehouse.

P. G. Wodehouse was the son of a British magistrate who was based in Hong Kong, disliked working in a bank, spent much of his early adult life in France, moved to New York and Hollywood and wrote some of the most keenly observed satire on upper-class English humour ever seen. His greatest and most successful creations were the delightfully amiable but idle and not always very bright Bertie Wooster and his highly competent valet Jeeves, who constantly rescued Bertie from the most awful scrapes. Their adventures were charted by Wodehouse in ten novels and some 30 short stories, running from the tale "Extricating Young Gussie", which he wrote in 1915, to the novel *Aunts Aren't Gentlemen* in 1974. Most remarkably, his style emerged fully formed from the outset and three things never changed over those 59 years: the superbly fluent manner with which Wodehouse played with the English language; the relentless humour with which he made fun of the English upper classes; and the tenderness with which he portrayed the relationship between Jeeves and Wooster, who clearly feel great affection for each other while maintaining the master–servant relationship.

As examples of Wodehouse's playful way with language, we might mention that he was the first English writer to use the word "cuckoo" to mean crazy and to use "cuppa" to refer to a cup of tea; he was the creator of the term "oojah-cum-spliff" to mean that something is fine; and the first to use the terms what-the-hell, right-ho, and not-at-all as verbs: "This telephone call was Aunt Dahlia what-the-helling"; "We became chummy. I asked her to marry me. She right-hoed"; "I was not-at-alling and shoving the handkerchief up my sleeve again". He also, in *Meet Mr Mulliner*, introduced the word "whiffled" to mean drunk. ("Intoxicated? The word did not express it by a mile. He was oiled, boiled, fried, plastered, whiffled, sozzled, and blotto.") Wodehouse was not, however, the first to use the word "lallapaloosa" (or "lollapalooza") to mean something outstandingly good, but he was the first British writer to import it from America.

Perhaps the single most inspired feature of his Jeeves and Wooster tales, however, was the brilliant trick of having Bertie narrate almost all the stories. Arthur Conan Doyle had employed a similar device in his Sherlock Holmes stories, where Watson was the one who explained what happened, but in those tales of detection, it makes sense because Watson is on a similar intellectual level to the readers so is better placed to communicate with them. Bertie, however, usually does not know what is going on and hearing his version of everything adds greatly to the comedy.

This aspect of the stories is very much diluted in their many television or film adaptations, but the hilarity of the tales and Wodehouse's use of language ensure that they survive the transition. Here are a dozen favourite examples of pure Wodehouse which are very funny in print or on-screen:

1.   "He had just about enough intelligence to open his mouth when he wanted to eat, but certainly no more." (*Tales of St Austin's*, 1903)

2.   "She looked away. Her attitude seemed to suggest that she had finished with him, and would be obliged if somebody would come and sweep him up." ("Ruth in Exile", from *The Man Upstairs and Other Stories*, 1914)

3.   "A melancholy-looking man, he had the appearance of one who has searched for the leak in life's gas-pipe with a lighted candle." ("The Man Who Disliked Cats", from *The Man Upstairs and Other Stories*, 1914)

4.   "One of the King Georges of England – I forget which – once said that a certain number of hours' sleep each

night – I cannot recall at the moment how many – made a man something which for the time being has slipped my memory." (*Something New*, 1915)

5. "I'm not absolutely certain of the facts, but I rather fancy it's Shakespeare who says that it's always just when a fellow is feeling particularly braced with things in general that Fate sneaks up behind him with the bit of lead piping." (*Jeeves and the Unbidden Guest*, 1916)

6. "And so the merry party began. It was one of those jolly, happy, bread-crumbling parties where you cough twice before you speak, and then decide not to say it after all." (*My Man Jeeves*, 1919)

7. "She fitted in my biggest arm-chair as if it had been built round her by someone who knew they were wearing arm-chairs tight about the hips that season." (*Carry On, Jeeves*, 1925)

8. "Marriage is not a process for prolonging the life of love, sir. It merely mummifies its corpse." (*The Small Bachelor*, 1927)

9. "The Right Hon. was a tubby little chap who looked like he had been poured into his clothes and had forgotten to say 'When'." (*Very Good, Jeeves*, 1930)

10. "Into the face of the young man who sat on the terrace of the Hotel Magnifique at Cannes there had crept a look of furtive shame, the shifty hangdog look which announces that an Englishman is about to speak French." (*The Luck of the Bodkins*, 1935)

11. "He spoke with a certain what-is-it in his voice, and I could see that, if not actually disgruntled, he was far from being gruntled." (*The Code of the Woosters*, 1938)

12. "It was one of those cases where you approve the broad, general principle of an idea but can't help being in a bit of a twitter at the prospect of putting it into practical effect. I explained this to Jeeves, and he said much the same thing had bothered Hamlet." (*Joy in the Morning*, 1946)

Once Wodehouse had stimulated Britain's appetite for humorous novels, other authors emerged or adapted their styles to feed it. None has ever matched Wodehouse's marvellous capacity to produce an unending stream of benign yet irrepressibly funny prose, but many have added something to contribute to the rise of British humour in the second half of the 20th century.

Kingsley Amis updated the basic type of storylines adopted by Smollett, Sterne and Fielding by bringing us in 1954 the tale of a modern hapless hero in Lucky Jim, whose love life and career as a lecturer at a minor university are equally disaster-prone. Amis also wrote *One Fat Englishman* (1963) which revealed to all of us the fact that "Outside every fat man there was an even fatter man trying to close in."

This may have paved the way for Anthony Burgess's trilogy of novels about another fat Englishman named Enderby, which included the following piece of linguistic gymnastics: "Then, instead of expensive mouthwash, he had breathed on Hogg-Enderby, bafflingly (for no banquet would serve, because of the known redolence of onions, onions) onions. 'Onions,' said Hogg." (*Enderby Outside*, 1968). Writing in 1982, Burgess cited this brilliantly ludicrous creation as the one thing he would most like to be remembered for. It was another of his Enderby novels, *Inside Mr Enderby*, however, in which, on the subject of laughter, he produced another of his most often quoted lines: "Laugh and the world laughs with you, snore and you sleep alone."

Both Amis and Burgess went on to highly successful literary careers after dipping their typewriters into the world of comic novels, but most later comic writers stuck to being amusing.

Between 1971 and 2010, Tom Sharpe produced several highly successful comic novels, the first two of which, *Riotous Assembly* and *Indecent Exposure* were set in his native South Africa and, as the titles may suggest, were vicious satires lampooning that country and its secret police and were the sort of scathing attack on state corruption that Wodehouse would never have even considered. Sharpe's later works, beginning with *Porterhouse Blue* in 1974, were mainly set in English academia and gloriously mock the atavistic out-of-touchness of dons at our finest universities.

Meanwhile, back in America, another novel came that was destined to become a comic classic. Joseph Heller's *Catch-22* was first published in 1961 when the Vietnam War had already been raging for six years. Yet Heller had started writing this satirical anti-war story in 1953 and it was set during the Second World War between 1942 and 1944.

The American television personality Steve Allen may have been the first to say "tragedy plus time equals comedy" but he did not offer guidelines on how much time it takes. The time between the end of the Second World War and the publication of *Catch-22* was 17 years; the time between the end of the Korean War and the original feature film *M*A*S*H**, which led to the successful TV series, was also 17 years, but neither of those was the first to lampoon war.

An earlier work that similarly made fun of military authorities was Jaroslav Hašek's *The Good Soldier Švejk* of which the first part was published in Prague in 1921. Josef Švejk, the hero of the story, is so eager to join up and serve the Austrian emperor in the war that he is declared insane and sent to a mental asylum. For the rest of the book, after he is freed to resume his military career, it becomes unclear who is madder: Švejk or his military commanders. As the full title *The Fateful Adventures of the Good Soldier Švejk During the World War* makes clear, the story is set during the war that ended in 1918, so in this case the time between tragedy and comedy was reduced to three years, but perhaps the First World War, despite its horrors, offered better opportunities for literary amusement than those that followed.

After this period of making serious fun of war, however, the comic emphasis shifted in the direction of science fiction and fantasy. Douglas Adams led the way with his *Hitchhiker's Guide to the Galaxy*, which began life as a radio series in 1978 but the following year became a highly successful book.

He gained a vast fan base through lines about spaceships such as: "Great big yellow somethings the size of office blocks. They hung in the air in exactly the same way that bricks don't." And: "There is an art to flying . . . or rather a knack. The knack lies in learning how to throw yourself at the ground and miss." And when one reads: "Time is an illusion, lunchtime doubly so", one is left with a sense of amazement that Groucho Marx did not say it first.

Adams died of a heart attack at the shockingly young age of 49 but his *Hitchhiker* books, which he described as "a trilogy in five parts" established a genre of gloriously funny fantasy/science fiction which quickly came to be dominated by three writers. The most famous and successful of these was Terry Pratchett, whose 40 *Discworld* fantasies earned him the devotion of a large band of followers.

There is a good argument, however, that Tom Holt is just as imaginative and has even better titles such as *Snow White and the Seven Samurai* and *Life, Liberty and the Pursuit of Sausages*. The best titles of all, however, are those of Robert Rankin. One has only to see the words *The Brentford Chainstore Massacre*, or *Raiders of the Lost Car Park*, or *Sex and Drugs and Sausage Rolls* and you know that the rest of the book will be comic mayhem. It was also Robert Rankin who pointed out, in *Web Site Story*, that the sexiest word in the English language is "plinth". His politically incorrect advice to anyone who does not realize this is to get a woman to say "plinth" slowly and watch her mouth as she does so.

With comic fiction led on such insane adventures, it must have come as a relief to many to be able to take refuge in the works of David Nobbs who, quite apart from being a scriptwriter for some of Britain's best loved comedians such as Kenneth Williams, Les Dawson and *The Two Ronnies* as well as those already mentioned, also brought realism back to comic novels. Just as Wodehouse had taken hugely affectionate aim at the English upper classes, Nobbs pinpointed the foibles of the middle class and their aspirations and disappointments. His great breakthrough came with *The Fall and Rise of Reginald Perrin*, which was turned into a hugely successful television serial starring Leonard Rossiter in the title role. Bored with his mundane existence, endless routine and dull job, Reggie fakes his own death and re-invents himself, coming back as someone totally different. Based on the inspired observation that there is a Reggie Perrin in all of us (well, all of us of a middle-class persuasion anyway) this was an inspired premise for a comic novel.

Whether they were about love (*Cupid's Dart*), life (*Going Gently*), food (*Pratt à Manger*), sexual reassignment (*Sex and Other Changes*) or other human problems, Nobbs's novels all displayed his deep insights into human nature, producing sympathy and laughter in equal measures.

His literary style was also beautiful and precise. Perhaps my favourite line comes at the start of the second chapter of his first novel, *The Itinerant Lodger*. I have always felt that with enough effort, anyone ought to be able to come up with something like "It was the best of times, it was the worst of times", or, "It was a bright cold day in April, and the clocks were striking thirteen", or even, "It is a truth universally acknowledged, that a single man in possession of a good fortune, must be in want of a wife", which as you probably know are the opening lines of *A Tale of Two Cities*, *Nineteen Eighty-Four* and *Pride and Prejudice*, but even if Charles Dickens, George Orwell and Jane Austen worked together on it, I very much doubt that they could have produced an opening sentence for chapter two as perfect as "The house was filled with the aura of impending stew."

As I hope this breathless romp through four centuries of comic novels has shown, the genre has grown in scope, complexity and sophistication, with the 20th century offering far greater choice for the reader than ever before; and, based on the evidence so far, the 21st century looks set to bring even greater joy and literary laughter. Two writers in particular have surpassed anything that went before in their mastery of comic inventiveness and style.

In 2009, the Swedish writer Jonas Jonasson brought out *The Hundred-Year-Old Man Who Climbed Out of the Window and Disappeared*, which tells the tale of Allan Karlsson who has no interest in the hundredth birthday party they are throwing for him at the old folks' home where he lives, so he climbs out of a window and escapes. Mixing his adventures with flashbacks over his long life, the book is a hilarious concoction, taking in most of the major events of the 20th century as well as having its own story to tell.

In 2013, *The Hundred-Year-Old Man* was turned into a successful film and in 2018 Jonasson published an equally funny sequel called *The Accidental Further Adventures of the Hundred-Year-Old Man*. He has also written the very funny and eventful *The Girl Who Saved the King of Sweden* (2012), and in 2015, the most hilarious yet, *Hitman Anders and the Meaning of it All*, which is about a thuggish hitman who sees the light and founds his own religion. Then in 2021, Jonasson's fifth novel, *Sweet, Sweet Revenge Ltd*, came out, further confirming that his comic inventiveness seems inexhaustible.

In 2016, however, a rival emerged to Jonas Jonasson for the title of funniest novelist on earth in the form of the American Amor Towles, whose *A Gentleman in Moscow* is not only a very funny book but one of the most precisely written comic novels ever, with every word deliciously chosen.

It tells the tale of Count Alexander Rostov and his determined attempts to remain a gentleman despite the brutality and ignorance of the Soviet regime that has come to power in his country. When the Count is moved to an attic room in his hotel, for example, we are told: "The Count stood and banged his head on the slope of the ceiling. 'Just so,' he replied." In another scene, he greets a pigeon pecking at the window with the words: "How good of you to stop by", then answers its repeated pecking with: "Ah yes. There is something in what you say." Only a true gentleman would talk in such a respectful manner to a ceiling and a pigeon, and the book is full of such gentlemanly turns of phrase.

The signs are propitious that this is going to be a great century for lovers of comic novels.

14

EINSTEIN'S PARROT

*"Common sense is actually nothing more than a deposit
of prejudices laid down in the mind prior to the age of
eighteen."*

Albert Einstein

I'm sorry to report that Long John Silver's parrot died today
of obesity. On the plus side, it's a huge weight off his shoulders.

In 2004, a document was found in an Albert Einstein archive
at Princeton University consisting of 62 pages of a diary kept
by Johanna Fantova between October 1953 and April 1956.
She had been a friend and companion of Einstein during his
final years and, as well as recording his thoughts about science
and politics, she revealed other surprising details including
his relationship with a parrot he had been given by a medical
institute as a present on his 75th birthday. Einstein called the
parrot Bibo and according to Fantova diagnosed it as suffering
from depression and tried to cheer it up by telling it bad jokes.
She says that the parrot recovered but promptly developed an
infection that it passed on to Einstein.

Sadly, she provided no information or clues as to the precise
jokes Einstein told the parrot, so further research has not been
performed on the potential medicinal value of jokes to depressed
parrots, but in recent years a good deal of evidence has been
found that humans and the great apes are not the only creatures
that laugh.

In the 1970s, young chimpanzees were observed to laugh when playing with each other, but a breakthrough in laughter research was made around 1997 as we mentioned in Chapter 7, when young rats were found to emit a high-pitched giggle when engaged in rough-and-tumble games. This had previously not been noticed because their giggling was far beyond the pitch that humans could hear, but once equipment began to be used to monitor it, the science of rat laughter developed rapidly.

The easiest way to induce giggling in young humans was known to be tickling, so researchers began tickling rats. A research team led by American-Estonian neuroscientist Jaap Panksepp ran a series of experiments that led to some surprising discoveries. One of the earliest provided an answer to the question of whether rats, like babies, don't respond to tickling if they are not in a ticklish mood. What Panksepp and his team did was to waft the smell of cats over some of the rats while tickling them and, sure enough, this interference with their emotional state put an end to their giggling.

By 2021, more than 70 scientific articles had been devoted to various aspects of rat tickling, including discussions of the best way to tickle rats and whether infant rats seem to like the same sort of tickling as human babies. In humans, two types of tickling had been identified: *knismesis*, which consists of a light touch or stroke evoking a shiver or a twitch, and *gargalesis*, which is a harder, more rhythmic probing leading to a more intense pleasure sensation. Rats responded to both types but seemed to like *gargalesis* more.

Perhaps the most remarkable rat-tickling experiments of all were carried out by three Polish researchers, Rafal Rygula, Helena Pluta and Piotr Popik at the Polish Academy of Sciences in Krakow, which were reported in the online science journal *PLOS ONE* in 2012 under the title "Laughing Rats Are Optimistic".

There were three stages to the experiment. Stage one: lab rats were divided into two groups. Rats in one group were tickled to make them laugh, while rats in the other group were just picked up to receive the same amount of handling, but no tickling. Stage two: the rats were placed in a box in front of a lever and were trained to distinguish between the sounds of two tones. If they pressed the lever after hearing one tone, they received a reward of food, but if they pressed the lever after the other tone, they were given an electric shock. They soon learned which was the good tone and which the bad. Stage three: they were played a tone that was halfway between the two they had heard before and the experimenters waited to see whether they pressed the lever or not.

The question was: would they be optimistic and press the lever or pessimistically leave it alone? The results showed that the rats who had been made happy by tickling were significantly more likely to press the lever than the unhappy, untickled rats.

In 2021, in *Bioacoustics*, the international journal of animal sound and its recording, Sasha Winkler and Gregory Bryant of UCLA published "Play vocalisations and human laughter: a comparative review", in which they listed 65 species that had been found to emit spontaneous vocal signals akin to human laughter. Just under half of these species were monkeys or apes, but as well as rats, the long list included, among others, one species each of sea lion, elk, gerbil, dog, slow loris, badger, mink, kangaroo, elephant and magpie, two species of wildcat, dolphin, fox and polecat, three species of mongoose and – I almost forgot – two species of parrots. So perhaps Einstein was on the right lines after all when he told jokes to his parrot, though tickling might have been a more effective way to treat its depression.

The idea of telling animals jokes, however, has perhaps understandably been given less attention than telling jokes to computers or getting computers to create their own jokes to tell us. In recent years, this has attracted increasing interest from the artificial intelligence community. Despite the increasing sophistication of allegedly smart applications such as Alexa and Siri, the linguistic challenges of humour continue to prove difficult to overcome.

The first serious attempts began around 1994 and it may be no coincidence that this was the same year that a computer chess program defeated the reigning world chess champion. Chess had long been a major goal for programmers, so when Chess Genius defeated Garry Kasparov, it was hailed as a large step forward for silicon-kind, even if it was in a quick-play event, which everyone knew gave computers an advantage. It was another three years before the IBM computer Deep Blue defeated Kasparov in a match played at a more normal slow rate of play, but the AI community had already turned its mind to the more significant problem of human language.

Compared with the problems set by programming a computer to play chess, getting one to understand language is massively more complex. Compared with calculating the future of at most 32 pieces arranged on 64 squares, following clear rules, the idea of permuting hundreds of thousands of words in a meaningful yet only partially rule-dictated manner is on a much higher level. The challenge of getting machines to understand and even produce jokes might have seemed a good place to start. Jokes are short and often follow known patterns according to an analysable scheme. Yet as a sub-domain of language, they pose a distinct problem for programmers: while the essence of most language is its logicality, jokes are inherently illogical or at least based on ambiguity. The standard technique of the joke-teller is to set up one natural interpretation of the words in the listener's mind and then derail that process at the last moment onto a separate track. The incongruity of the derailment is what makes it funny. Getting a computer to do this, however, is a big problem as it has difficulties even ascribing a single meaning to a sentence in natural language.

One of the earliest attempts to get computers to write a very limited type of joke was described in the paper "An Implemented Model of Punning Riddles" in 1994 by Kim Binsted and Graeme Ritchie of Edinburgh University Artificial Intelligence Department. They begin with the very reasonable assertion that a suitable goal for AI research is to get a computer to do "a task which, if done by a human, requires intelligence to perform", and point out that in that respect, "the production of humorous texts, including jokes and riddles, is a fit topic for AI research", With that in mind, they explain their production of JAPE, the Joke Analysis and Production Engine designed to produce riddles from a limited vocabulary of ambiguous or punning words.

As Binsted and Ritchie admitted, however, JAPE "succeeds in generating pieces of text that are recognizably jokes, but some of them are not very good jokes". Even when an improved version of JAPE was produced in 2008 with the wince-inducing elaborate acronym of STANDUP (System To Augment Non-speakers' Dialogue Using Puns), the jokes it produced were still more likely to induce groans than laughs, for example: "What is the difference between a pretty glove and a silent cat? One is a cute mitten, the other is a mute kitten"; or "What do you get when you cross a frog with a road? A main toad." And those were listed among the better jokes produced by the software. Its poorer efforts were largely unintelligible or totally unfunny, often both.

In 2006, the Dutch computer scientist Anton Njiholt identified the real problem in writing software to generate good jokes: "General humour understanding and the closely related area of natural-language understanding require an understanding of rational and social intelligence, so we won't be able to solve these problems until we've solved all AI problems."

One of the major problems in this area is that poor as computers may be at creating jokes, part of the reason is that they are just as bad at differentiating between good jokes and bad jokes. If this were not so, they could assess their own creations and reject the bad ones. However, an interesting success was reported in 2019 in a paper titled "Making Sense of Recommendations" in the *Journal of Behavioral Decision Making* by a team led by Michael Yeomans of the Harvard Business School. The research behind it was motivated by the rapid increase in recent years of consumer recommendations to individuals based on computer analysis of data about their past behaviour. Yeomans's idea was to see whether computers could analyse a person's taste in jokes and use that to predict which jokes that person would find funniest.

The results showed not only that such predictions could indeed be made, but that they are better than similar predictions made by people who know the subject well. The experimental design was clever but simple: subjects first had to rate each of a preliminary set of jokes on a scale of -10 (not funny at all) to +10 (very funny indeed). The computer then analysed their results and made predictions on how each subject would rate a further set of jokes. The subjects' partners predicted how they thought the new jokes would be rated and both sets of predictions were then compared with the actual ratings given by the subjects. And the computer predictions were found to be significantly more accurate. Even when this was pointed out to the subjects, however, they still said they would place more faith in recommendations from other people than from artificial intelligence.

Computers, it seems, may not know much about jokes, but they have ways of finding out what we like.

And finally, as they like to say on news broadcasts to introduce an item less weighty than others that have been discussed, here is a serious piece of advice from J. B. Morton when he was criticized for laughing at his own Beachcomber columns. I think it offers better advice on the perception of humour than any philosopher has ever managed:

I bellow with laughter when I get a good joke. Why shouldn't I? A man who doesn't laugh at his own jokes is timid, self-conscious and altogether half-strangled with beastliness. It is argued that this is a sign of conceit. Bosh. It is a sign of being able to enjoy oneself without consulting the conventions of the half-men. So laugh and be damned to the world.

EPILOGUE

"Laughter is not at all a bad beginning for a friendship, and it is far the best ending for one."

Oscar Wilde, *The Picture of Dorian Gray*

Q: Why did the introduction and the conclusion break up?
A: They were just never on the same page . . .

As I said in the introduction all those chapters ago, the best reason for writing a book is because you want to read it, so now is the moment to decide what, if anything, we have learned about humour and whether it has been worthwhile.

Well, I suppose we have learned that Plato was quite wrong about humour and Aristotle was wrong to have doubts about it. We have learned that new jokes are, on the whole, better than old jokes, even when we take into account the fact that we are less likely to have heard them before, and we have learned that various Churches have got themselves into real philosophical tangles over the merits of humour.

We may well have decided that there is very little hope of anyone coming up soon with a Grand Unified Theory of Humour (GUT-Humour), but if they do so, the many fMRI scans currently being performed on the brains of people who are looking at cartoons will probably have played a big role in the discovery.

Since the impact of humour diminishes on repetition, our sense of humour must necessarily evolve, whether we are talking about an individual's humour or that of the culture of the nation or community in which they live. Whether we are talking about spoken jokes, written jokes, or jokes performed or transmitted on radio, television or in theatres, all the evidence is that the world is getting funnier and more sophisticated – though some jokes seem timeless.

Over the past few years, several surveys have reported that people trust comedians to be more honest than politicians or even corporate-controlled newsreaders. Thanks to presenters such as Stephen Colbert, Jon Stewart and Trevor Noah on Comedy Central's *The Daily Show* on US television, or Paul Merton and Ian Hislop on *Have I Got News For You* on BBC television in the UK, or almost anyone on BBC radio in *The News Quiz*, more and more people are choosing humour as a source of reliable information. As Jon Stewart put it himself in an interview on Fox News in 2011: "The embarrassment is that I'm given credibility in this world because of the disappointment that the public has in what the news media does", and that perhaps more than anything explains the massive lure of comedy as a source of information.

So despite the suspicions and hostility shown toward humour over many centuries from various organizations and powerful, self-elected individuals, and the efforts of a po-faced, bigoted, humourless, unsmiling, self-important minority to control, censor or even ban humour has, for the moment at least, lost the battle.

As we prepare to enjoy the funniest, most confident, most creative, most relaxed and wittiest jokes, films, television and books of humour's long and troubled history in the years to come, let us give the last words to William Blake from his *Songs of Innocence and Experience*, first published in 1789. Now there was someone who really understood the importance and joy of laughter:

The Laughing Song

When the green woods laugh with the voice of joy,
And the dimpling stream runs laughing by;
When the air does laugh with our merry wit,
And the green hill laughs with the noise of it;

When the meadows laugh with lively green,
And the grasshopper laughs in the merry scene;
When Mary and Susan and Emily
With their sweet round mouths sing "Ha ha he!"

When the painted birds laugh in the shade,
Where our table with cherries and nuts is spread:
Come live, and be merry, and join with me,
To sing the sweet chorus of "Ha ha he!"

NOTES

Just in case anyone wants further information about the sources of some books, articles and quotation referred to in the text, here they are, chapter by chapter:

Epigraph quotation
From a television review by Clive James in *The Observer*, 4 February 1979

Introduction
Scott Weems is the author of *Ha! The Science of When We Laugh and Why* (2014). The quotation comes from an article "How comedy makes us better people" by Mary O'Hara in BBC Future, August 2016.

Mary Ann Shaffer: from *The Guernsey Literary and Potato Peel Pie Society* (2008), p. 22.

Gil Greengross et al., *Journal of Evolutionary Psychology*, 2008.

Encyclopaedia Britannica (1997), Vol. 6, entry on "Humour".

Sigmund Freud, *International Journal of Psycho-Analysis*, 9(1), 1928.

Leif Kennair et al., *Evolutionary Psychology*, 2022.

Alan Roberts, *A Philosophy of Humour*, Springer, 2019.

Isaac Asimov, "Jokester" first appeared in the December 1956 issue of *Infinity Science Fiction.*

Part One: Humour in Theory
Richard Feynman, from his lecture series at Cornell University in 1964.

Chapter 1: New Jokes for Old
Ludwig Wittgenstein, quoted in *Ludwig Wittgenstein: A Memoir* by Norman Malcolm, 1958 and 1984, OUP, p. 28 in second edition.

George Vasey, *The Philosophy of Laughter and Smiling*, J. Burns, London, 1875.

Chapter 2: Do Gods Laugh?
Hennie A. J. Kruger, *Laughter in the Old Testament,* In die Skriflig/In Luce Verbi, February 2014.

Umberto Eco, *The Name of the Rose*, first published as *Il Nome Della Rosa* in Italian in 1980, English translation by William Weaver published in 1983.

Karl-Heinz Ott and Bernard Schweitzer, "Does religion shape people's sense of humour?", *European Journal of Humour Research*, 6(1), 2018, pp. 12–35.

Chapter 3: No Laughing Matter
Thomas Hobbes, *Leviathan*, London, 1651.

Bertrand Russell, *An Outline of Intellectual Rubbish: a hilarious catalogue of organized and individual stupidity*, Haldeman-Julius Publications, 1943.

Anthony Ashley-Cooper, 3rd Earl of Shaftesbury, *Essay on the Freedom of Wit and Humour*, London, 1709.

Herbert Spencer, *The Physiology of Laughter*, Macmillan, 1860.

James Beattie, *An Essay on Laughter, and Ludicrous Composition*, written in 1774 and published in 1776.

Arthur Schopenhauer, *The World as Will and Idea*, originally published in Leipzig as *Die Welt als Wille und Vorstellung*, 1818.

Henri Bergson, *Laughter: An Essay on the Meaning of the Comic*, originally published in 1900 as *Le Rire, Essai sur la signification du comique*.

Arthur Koestler, *The Act of Creation*, Hutchinson, London 1964.

Thomas Veatch, "A Theory of Humor", *Humor: International Journal of Humor Research*, 11(2), May 1998, pp. 161–216.

Peter McGraw and Caleb Warren, "Benign Violations: Making Immoral Behavior Funny", *Physiological Science*, 21(8), 2010, pp. 1141–1149.

Matthew Hurley, Daniel Dennett and Reginald B. Adams Jr, *Inside Jokes*, MIT Press, 2011.

John Godfrey Saxe, "The Blind Men and the Elephant", first published in *The Poems of John Godfrey Saxe*, J. Osgood, Boston, 1872.

Neil Simon, *The Sunshine Boys*, premiered on Broadway, 20 December 1972, with Jack Albertson and Sam Levene in the leading roles, filmed in 1975 with George Burns and Walter Matthau.

Tom Stoppard, *Professional Foul*, broadcast in the BBC *Play of the Week* series on 21 September 1977.

Chapter 4: Laughter and Humour

Samuel Johnson, *Life of Cowley,* part of his Lives of the English Poets series published by Cassell & Company, 1779–91.

Robert Provine, "Laughter", *American Scientist*, 84, Jan–Feb 1996.

Paul Carus, "On The Philosophy of Laughing", *The Monist*, 8(2), 1898, pp. 250–272.

Chapter 5: A Psychologist Walked Into a Bar...

Thomas Aquinas, *Summa Theologica*, Benziger Brothers, 1485, first published in English translation in 1911.

Sigmund Freud, *Der Witz und seine Beziehung zum Unbewußten*, Leipzig 1905, translated into English as *Jokes and Their Relation to the Unconscious*, Routledge & Kegan Paul, 1960.

Chapter 6: All in the Mind

R. S. Wyer and J. E. Collins, "A Theory of Humor Elicitation", *Psychological Review*, 99(4), 1992, pp. 663–688.

Vinod Goel and Raymond J. Dolan, "The functional anatomy of humor: segregating cognitive and affective components", *Nature Neuroscience*, 4(3), 2001, pp. 237–238.

Joseph M. Moran, William Kelley et al., "Neural Correlates of Humor Detection and Appreciation", *Journal of Neuroimage*, 21(3), March 2004, pp. 1055–1060.

K. K. Watson, B. J. Matthews, J. M. Allman, "Brain Activation during Sight Gags and Language-Dependent Humor", *Cerebral Cortex*, March 2006 (published online).

O. Amir, and I. Biederman, "The neural correlates of humor creativity", *Frontiers in Human Neuroscience*, 10, 2016.

Robert Frost: the quotation at the end of the chapter appears thousands of times on the Internet and was perhaps first attributed to the poet Frost in the *Oxford Dictionary of Medical Quotations*, 2004, p. 37.

Chapter 7: Evolution
Johann Huizinga: *Homo Ludens* (1938 in Dutch), translated into English as *Homo Ludens, a study of the play element in culture* (1955).

Michael Brecht and Shimpei Ishiyama, "Neural correlates of ticklishness in the rat somatosensory cortex", *Science*, 354, 2016, pp. 757–760.

Charles Darwin, *The Expression of the Emotions in Man and Animals*, John Murray, London, 1872, p. 201.

Guillaume Duchenne de Boulogne, *Mécanisme de la physionomie humaine*, Veuve Jules Renouard, Paris, 1862.

James Beattie, *Essays on Poetry and Music: As They Affect the Mind: On Laughter, and Ludicrous Composition*, 1779.

Ricky Gervais, "The Difference Between American and British Humour," *Time* magazine, 9 November 2011.

Harold Nicolson, *The English sense of humour: An essay* (Dropmore essays, no.1), 1946.

John Locke, *Essay Concerning Human Understanding*, London, 1689.

Thomas Hobbes, *Elements of Law, Natural and Politic*, London 1640.

Chapter 8: Comedians
Henry Louis Mencken, *A Book of Burlesques,* John Lane Company, 1916.

Joseph Strutt, *The Sports and Pastimes of the People of England,* Methuen and Co., 1801.

Philip Stubbes, *Anatomie of Abuses*, London, 1583.

Chapter 9: Theatre
John Dryden, *Essay Of Dramatick Poesy*, 1668.

Michael Burden, "Pots, privies and WCs; crapping at the opera in London before 1830", *Cambridge Opera Journal*, 23(1–2), 2011, pp. 27–50.

Tracy C. Davis, "Filthy – nay Pestilential: Sanitation and Victorian Theatres", in *Exceptional Spaces: Essays in Performance and History*, ed. Della Pollock, University of North Carolina Press, 1998.

Jennifer Terni, "A Genre for Early Mass Culture: French Vaudeville and the City, 1830–1848", *Theatre Journal*, 58, 2006, pp. 221–248.

Marie Lloyd, "The Music Hall War 1907", quoted in Midge Gillies, *Marie Lloyd: The One and Only*, Orion Publishing, 1999.

Georges Feydeau, quoted in Peter Meyer, *Feydeau*, London, Oberon, 2003.

Chapter 10: Cinema
Charlie Chaplin, quoted in *Chicago Tribune*, 6 April 1972.

Harold Lloyd, quoted in *Motion Picture*, 1936.

Chapter 12: Cartoons

Mark O'Donnell, *Elementary Education: An Easy Alternative to Actual Learning,* Random House,1985.

"The Making of *The Simpsons:* The Art of Bart", *Entertainment Weekly*, May 1990, pp. 36–43.

Bruce Handy, *Time* magazine online Q&A session, 4 June 1998.

Chapter 14: Einstein's Parrot

Albert Einstein: the quotation at the start of the chapter appears in "The Universe and Dr Einstein", a series in *Life* magazine, and later a book of the same title by Lincoln Barnett in 1948.

Kim Binsted and Graeme Ritchie, *An Implemented Model of Punning Riddles*, AAAI-94 Proceedings, 1994.

Anton Njiholt: "Embodied conversational agents: A little humor too", *IEEE Intelligent Systems*, 21(2), 2006, pp. 62–64.

Michael Yeomans et al., "Making Sense of Recommendations", *Journal of Behavioral Decision Making*, 2019, pp. 403–414.

INDEX